MULTICULTURAL FOUNDATIONS OF PSYCHOLOGY AND COUNSELING

Series Editors: Allen E. Ivey and Derald Wing Sue

Multicultural Encounters:
Case Narratives from a Counseling Practice
Stephen Murphy-Shigematsu

Community Genograms:
Using Individual, Family, and Cultural Narratives with Clients
Sandra A. Rigazio-DiGilio, Allen E. Ivey,
Kara P. Kunkler-Peck, and Lois T. Grady

D0792704

Community Genograms

Using Individual, Family, and Cultural Narratives with Clients

SANDRA A. RIGAZIO-DiGILIO

ALLEN E. IVEY

KARA P. KUNKLER-PECK

LOIS T. GRADY

contributing author
ANTHONY J. RIGAZIO-DIGILIO

foreword by
DOROTHY S. BECVAR

TEACHERS
COLLEGE
PRESS

Teachers College
Columbia University
New York and London

Published by Teachers College Press, 1234 Amsterdam Avenue, New York, NY 10027

Library of Congress Cataloging-in-Publication Data

Community genograms : using individual, family, and cultural narratives with clients /
    Sandra A. Rigazio-DiGilio . . . [et al.] ; foreword by Dorothy S. Becvar.
        p. cm. — (Multicultural foundations of psychology and counseling)
    Includes bibliographical references and index.
    ISBN 0-8077-4554-5 (cloth : alk. paper) — ISBN 0-8077-4553-7 (pbk. : alk. paper)
    1. Family psychotherapy—Technique. 2. Behavioral assessment—Charts,
diagrams, etc. 3. Narrative therapy. 4. Cultural psychiatry. 5. Community
psychology. I. Rigazio-DiGilio, Sandra A. II. Series.

    RC488.53.C65 2004
    616.89'156—dc22

                                                                            2004062080

ISBN 0-8077-4553-7 (paper)
ISBN 0-8077-4554-5 (cloth)

Printed on acid-free paper

Manufactured in the United States of America

12 11 10 09 08 07 06 05   8 7 6 5 4 3 2 1

Contents

Foreword

The latter decades of the twentieth century were characterized by an increase in awareness among mental health professionals of the need for much greater sensitivity to the larger cultural contexts in which individuals and families live and within which the problems they experience emerge. Called to task by both feminists and proponents of postmodernism for a view soon recognized to be far too narrow, counselors and therapists began to understand the importance of widening the lenses through which clients were viewed. Of crucial importance was the need to acknowledge the degree to which factors such as gender, ethnicity, power, and privilege participated in the creation of realities as well as in the ability to facilitate meaningful change.

Accordingly, a movement to enhance multicultural sensitivity and competence gradually evolved, culminating, in part, in various revised approaches to the therapeutic process. One response took the form of metaframeworks that aimed at highlighting various contextual issues and allowed for individualized responses that were sensitive to the unique characteristics of each client system, for example, those created by Breunlin, Schwartz, and MacKune-Karrer (1992) and Rigazio-DiGilio (1994). Similarly, several efforts have been made to expand the traditional genogram (Guerin & Pendagast, 1976; McGoldrick, Gerson, & Shellenberger, 1999), long considered an extremely useful tool for mapping family characteristics over three or more generations. Thus, some versions focus on religion and spirituality (Frame, 2000), one aims at understanding money issues (Mumford & Weeks, 2003), and others seek to recognize specific cultural dimensions (Congress, 1994; Hardy & Laszloffy, 1995).

While each of the above approaches represents an important contribution to the goal of increased contextual sensitivity, the authors of *Community Genograms* are to be congratulated for moving this development to another level. As a function of the potential of the community genogram to portray the issues of importance to each client and to do so in a manner appropriate for that client, counselors and therapists are being provided with a tool that may enhance their ability to understand the particular contextual characteristics impinging upon those with whom they are working. What is more, given that the community genogram is process oriented, it may be incorporated easily into the work of mental health professionals having widely differing theoretical orientations.

In this very pragmatic book, the community genogram is presented and illustrated in a manner consistent with a coconstructivist perspective. As readers are guided to a place of understanding, they are likely to be intrigued by the ways in which use of the community genogram may allow clients' stories to be viewed and reviewed at various points in time, both past and present, and in various ways, with the opportunity then to expand these stories into more comfortable futures. Aspects of these narratives that otherwise might have been overlooked are allowed to emerge as both figure and ground are considered, utilizing the client's perspective as organizing framework. What may be even more significant is that the authors have provided an avenue for creative expression should that be desired, while at the same time offering a standard format that may be adapted by clients to fit their situations should the former option seem too daunting. In either case, the community genogram allows for an operationalization of the postmodern emphasis on shared expertise as clients are encouraged to depict and narrate their life stories in ways that are most meaningful to them. Given such a combination of distinctive and unique characteristics, this book truly represents a noteworthy accomplishment.

DOROTHY S. BECVAR, PH.D.

Preface:
The Community Genogram

The community genogram is an assessment and treatment strategy that facilitates the understanding of individuals and families in social and historical context. We hope you will find that the community genogram provides a rich source of data, enabling you and your clients to understand how concerns, problems, and issues develop over time and across contexts.

Equally important, you will find the community genogram an invaluable source of client strengths. We argue that counseling and therapy, whether individual, family, or group centered, tend to focus predominantly on client difficulty and so-called pathology. Lasting change, however, builds on client, family, and community strength and capacity. As such, the various questioning strategies associated with constructing community genograms can guide you and your clients to maintain a focus on positive individual, family, and community strengths and resources.

Helping clients realize the many sources of strength they can access within themselves and within their wider community needs to be a part of every counseling or group session (Ivey, Gluckstern, & Ivey, 1992; Ivey, Pedersen, & Ivey, 2001). Community genogram approaches emphasize strengths within the positive orientation of narrative therapy. Clients learn to broaden the lens they use to rewrite and story their lives in stronger, more constructive, and more beneficial ways. We say, "If you cannot find something right about your client, then refer!"

The community genogram helps us, as clinicians, to see the individual or family client as part of a larger temporal and contextual community. This idea is akin to an African worldview, where "the idea of communal interconnection . . . not only promotes and supports the idea of persons within community, but also maintains that the vantage point grounded in community creates a more holistic conception of the *person as community*. . . . [In this regard] the sickness of the individual [or family] is symptomatic of a deeper communal malaise" (Ogbonnaya, 1994, p. 81).

"To deal with the symptom is at most a temporary benefit; real healing requires the establishment of right relationship [between persons and community]." Therefore, "when dealing with any 'pathology' the cultural dimensions influencing the individual's [or family's] concept of illness and behavior responses to crises should be taken seriously so that sociological and cultural ideas which play a significant role in the development and interaction of the [individual or collective] personality can become part of the therapeutic process." Finally, "in the communitarian process of healing, one cannot be 'saved' as an individual. . . . To heal the one, the many must also be healed or the one continues to be sick and to create sickness" (Ogbonnaya, 1994, p. 86).

TOWARD A COMMUNITY SPIRIT

One reason for writing this book was our desire to reinforce the value of community. In a time when many of us are reporting the lack of community in our busy lives, we need methods to help identify the community influences that can combine to improve or impede our pursuit of happiness. The activities depicted in this book demonstrate how to infuse these vital community influences into the counseling process. Often our clients are unaware of the power of these influences and how, if at all, they may make changes in their social environment. The focus of this book is to map these forces, whether in the past, the present or the future, to increase the levels of support our clients can use to initiate and sustain the changes they wish to create in their lives.

Bringing in community issues can often overwhelm both client and therapist. It is often easier to remain focused on the intrapersonal thoughts, feelings, and beliefs our clients bring to treatment. When large segments of the community are brought into treatment it may be difficult to retain a focused exploration of these broad, all-encompassing aspects of life. The community genogram allows our clients to determine which slices of the community will be salient and provides clear parameters to maintain the focus of this discussion.

It is through the analysis of community issues that our clients can reap two benefits. First, they may understand the community issues that contributed to their current situation. In this way, clients may feel empowered if they realize the external forces that colluded to oppress and minimize personal options available to them. Second, they may realize methods of altering community forces for themselves and others. It is this second benefit that may result in creating more optimizing environments for our clients and their wider communities. Certainly, many more people will benefit from changes in social services and policies that promote mental health for all. If we persist in helping one client at a time, we will never achieve the kind of social environments that honor individual differences and celebrate the interconnectedness of all community members.

CASE MATERIAL

Throughout this book we have liberally used interviews with clinical and nonclinical individuals, couples, and families to illustrate how the community genogram can be used to help clients analyze and act upon external influences that have affected their lives. The cases and interviews demonstrate a wide range of cultures, age groups, and clinical and lifespan issues. By examining the variety of questioning strategies contained in these examples, clinicians can derive methods of coconstructing community genograms. All personal identifying information has been changed to protect the privacy of those who have contributed to this book.

The examples offer a wide range of scenarios and variations of the community genogram. In the clinical cases, the approach is similar in that each intervention is aimed at empowering clients to understand and, eventually, influence the community forces that are operating in their immediate life space. Of course, other therapeutic methods aimed at more intrapersonal and intrafamilial issues were used, but these are not the focus of this book.

PRACTICE EXERCISES

In Chapters 2–4, practice exercises and practice questions are offered for you to use on yourself or to use with clients. The exercises and questions are provided to help create sufficient knowledge for clinicians to adapt the community genogram to their practice. We strongly urge you to fully participate in the exercises to experience the power of the community genogram and to use this knowledge to help clients sort through the many memories that are generated by these techniques. Feel free to alter these methods and questions to fit both the needs of your clientele and your ability to use visual, interactive devices in counseling and therapy.

RELEASING CLIENT CREATIVITY

We have found the creativity of our clients to be limitless, and we often learn new approaches and deeper questions to pursue as clients add their own insight and artistic preferences to the construction of their community genogram. We have tried to communicate the creativity and enthusiasm our clients have expressed when using a simple tool to unlock complex issues like community influences, supports, and obstacles. It is up to mental health professionals to help make the invisible forces influencing their clients visible. The community genogram is one tool, and we hope you and your clients find it as enjoyable and illuminating as our clients have.

Throughout the book, various examples of how clients have used their creativity and expressive skills to illustrate the complexities of community influences are presented. The variations demonstrate the unique configuration a community genogram can take to help clients isolate and explore contextual elements of their issues. We begin with a wide distribution of community genogram types in the early chapters of the book. In Chapter 3 a particular type of community genogram format, the *star diagram*, is introduced and then elaborated on in subsequent chapters. This decision was made for educative reasons and is not meant to limit your own or your client's creativity in depicting relevant contextual factors and interactions. Our central focus is to demonstrate how contextual dimensions contribute to the definition of and solution to clients' presenting issues, and this book is meant to be only a guide for designing activities and strategies that help clients assess the power of their community and devise ways to create change at both a personal and a community level.

OVERVIEW OF THE BOOK

It is impossible to include all the ways communities interact with individuals and families in one book. We have organized this book into six chapters that provide windows on how to relate contextual and cultural dimensions to personal and familial narratives. Chapter 1 provides an overview of the community genogram process and situates this tool within the domain of graphic assessment devices. It presents a broad overview and anchors our work within an ecosystemic framework. In Chapter 2 the specifics of how to construct community genograms is provided. We offer a multidimensional definition of self and family, and use this as a basis for introducing contextual issues into the treatment process. Chapter 3 offers a culturally informed perspective of human interaction and specifically focuses on the issues of boundaries and power. Both of these aspects are crucial in understanding how community and contextual variables influence clients' identity and the types of solutions they seek. Chapter 4 explores issues across the life span. Using a broad definition of the types of issues clients may present, we examine the potential differences persons may experience as they progress through life. In Chapter 5 a detailed analysis of one session is provided. Our goal here is to demonstrate the nuances of using a community genogram to explore issues of identity, power, and oppression. Chapter 6 provides a similar analysis, this time using a relational system, and shows the ways community genograms can assist families to understand the history of intergenerational dynamics and to influence the future unfolding of these dynamics. The epilogue concludes this work with suggestions on how to continue to use the community genogram in the service of client assessment, treatment, and evaluation. Each chapter offers a unique slice of how the community genogram can be used. When taken as a whole, the book creates a broad view that will assist clinicians to use the tools as they see fit in the particulars of their own practice.

A STEP CLOSER

By moving toward the integration of culture and counseling approaches, we hope this book helps move the field one step closer toward truly treating all clients with respect for the numerous contextual forces that shape client functioning. Rather than continuing the trend to blame the victims, the approach advocated in this book asks clinicians to search beyond the client's intrapsychic and interpersonal relationships to consider how community and intergenerational factors might figure in the manifestation and maintenance of distressed feelings, thoughts, and behavior. We do not believe that all client issues are initiated in wider contexts, but we do believe that the reaction of the wider community can ameliorate or exacerbate client issues. By identifying and linking community-based assets, our clients can realize new options for growth and change. This is the goal of our book: to help clients find relational, community, and cultural assets to enhance their lives.

Acknowledgments

Sandra respectfully acknowledges the influence and guidance of Allen Ivey in her training, career, and life. I am honored to collaborate with him on a project that brings culture, context, and multiperspective thought to the foreground of the therapeutic process. I also wish to thank Lois and Kara for the vision and clarity they brought to this project, and the individuals and families whose community genograms provide the real life translation of this work to practice. The professionals at Teachers College Press are to be commended for their assistance as this book came into being, especially the direction and support of Carol Collins. Finally, I wish to acknowledge my mother and father, in memory, and Anthony, Elizabeth, Nicholas, and Nonni, with love.

Allen gives special thanks to Mary Bradford Ivey for her constant support, editing, and encouragement. It has been a delight to know and work with Sandra Rigazio-DiGilio these past years and learn from and with her. Kara Kunkler-Peck and Lois Grady have been special stars of competence, and I feel lucky to be in partnership with them.

Kara expresses her gratitude to her coauthors for their dedication to the book and the ideas contained within. It has been a tremendous honor to have an opportunity to work with such a committed group of professionals. I would like to extend my deepest thanks to all my family members who have provided inspiration, encouragement, and support.

Lois gratefully acknowledges the support and mentorship of Allen Ivey during and after her pursuit of her doctorate. Doris Shallcross shepherded me through this doctorate. Elaine Anderson has been and is my special friend and constant support. Sandra Rigazio-DiGilio has been a fun and wonderful coauthor. Lyle Perkins inspired and mentored me for my Ceramic degree. Don Wise has been and is a teacher, mentor, coauthor, and colleague in my love of geology. I am also appreciative of the tolerance, continuing support, and encouragement for all the various interests in my life from my husband and children.

CHAPTER 1

The Community Genogram: Understanding Clients in Their Communities

This book introduces the community genogram as a therapeutic tool that can be used as both an interactive assessment and intervention strategy with individuals and families. The objective of this book is to consider clients as *individuals-in-relation* and as *families-in-relation* rather than as isolated entities. The community genogram emphasizes individual, relational, contextual, and cultural dimensions. It enables clinicians to see, in visual form, clients' perceived social networks of the past and present, as well as their anticipated future networks. The primary value of this strategy is that it facilitates the identification and activation of contextual and community dynamics and resources often times beyond the awareness of the clinician and client.

Three major points are raised in this chapter:

- **The definition of the community genogram**
- **The relationship of the community genogram to other graphic assessment tools**
- **How to use the community genogram within the counseling process**

The community genogram offers a natural, yet systematic, way to examine the impact of significant people, situations, and experiences that have affected clients and their sense of themselves. Community genograms are highly versatile and free up clients to select different time spans, contexts, and sets of people to explore at multiple points throughout the therapeutic relationship. There are endless modifications that can be made to the basic community genogram format and questioning strategies in order to integrate this device across all treatment modalities: individual, family, network, and consultation. Although certain elements of how community genograms are constructed and used will be common across all clients, how particular clients choose to represent important aspects of their lives will be more influenced by the particular constellation of issues they bring to treatment and by their own creative capacities and experiences.

The community genogram is a graphic assessment device used to surface and explore family, social, and cultural forces that influence individual and family development. Its aim is to help clients examine individual or family issues within their full contextual background. It focuses on important social (family, peer, and coworker) and community (church, school, neighborhood, municipal services) resources that may contribute to the client's problem and play a role in possible solutions. It is a versatile tool that can be used to capture different perspectives from family members and different time spans.

The community genogram is derived from two concepts. First, the term genogram is used to reinforce the importance of family legacies on the physical and psychological development of individuals and families. In traditional models of counseling and therapy, these legacies are often only examined in a decontextualized fashion. To place those legacies within the wider dynamic field generated by interaction with peer, ethnic, religious, and professional networks, the second concept of community setting is added. Through the community genogram, clients can depict the representations of key periods in their life that can support and deepen the therapeutic conversation.

Different from the more standardized techniques of family genograms (i.e., McGoldrick, Gerson, & Shellenberger, 1999), the community-oriented approach encourages clients to develop a broad image of self, family, and community in a way that is most helpful to them. As such, many variations on community genograms are possible with examples presented throughout this book.

GRAPHIC ASSESSMENT DEVICES: VISUALIZING THE HIDDEN STRUCTURE OF OUR LIVES

For several decades, graphically representing client experience has been acknowledged as an invaluable therapeutic tool (see Guerin & Pendagast, 1976; L'Abate & Bagarozzi, 1993; McGoldrick et al., 1999; Thomlison, 2002). Such strategies assist clinicians and clients alike to describe and reflect upon issues such as individual development and family dynamics.

The Family Genogram

The most common graphic assessment tool, the family genogram (McGoldrick et al., 1999), has been used in individual, family, group, and medical settings. The use of this device in gathering pertinent information in individual and family therapy has been a standard practice for many years.

The family genogram offers a comprehensive way to gather general information such as the names of significant family members and the dates of significant family events, like marriages, births, divorces, and deaths. Additionally, the way family genograms are organized can uncover valuable clinical information about issues such as family alliances, coalitions, and triangles; family legacies; and repeating family themes and scripts. Particularly useful for bringing out latent and unrecognized intergenerational family patterns, the family genogram demonstrates the value of systematically representing family data in a way that can be referred to at a glance by clinicians, clients, supervisors, and other human service professionals (see Becvar & Becvar, 2003: Dunn & Levitt, 2000; Frame, 2000; Gladding, 2002; Green, 2003; Green, 1999; Worden, 2003).

The Cultural Genogram

As more attention is given to ensuring the cultural competence of counselors and therapists, graphic assessment devices have been developed as concrete tools to assist in this process. The cultural genogram (Hardy & Laszloffy, 1995) is one of the more useful tools used for this purpose. The goal, as described by Hardy and Laszloffy, is to "promote cultural awareness and sensitivity by helping trainees to understand their cultural identities" (p. 228). This graphic organizer is used to (1) clarify the influence of culture on a family system; (2) identify significant groups that contribute to the formation of a cultural identity; (3) facilitate discussion that uncovers and challenges culturally based assumptions and stereotypes and unresolved culturally based conflicts; and (4) assist counselor and therapy students and supervisees to understand how their own cultural identities affect their therapeutic style and effectiveness (Hardy & Laszloffy, 1995).

Although the cultural genogram was conceived as a training tool, it also has clinical applicability (Congress, 1994). For example, it offers a framework that could be used to assist cross-cultural families whose symptoms manifest their attempt to blend or balance cultural issues.

The Eco-map

The eco-map is a paper-and-pencil and computer-generated simulation that graphically illustrates the relationships between individual and family clients within their environmental contexts (Hartman, 1978). The eco-map portrays the major systems, such as health care, social services, school, work, friends, and extended family members, that directly impact on the life space of the client. Lines and arrows connecting the client with these other systems represent various levels of conflict and support. Clinicians have used the eco-map as a tool for activating the client's participation in determining assessment, planning, and intervention strategies over the course of treatment (Gladding,

2002; Thomlison, 2002). Further, the eco-map has proved to be useful in helping clients realize the environmental stressors impacting on their situations and to identify alternative relationships and resources that might be helpful (Hanson & Boyd, 1996).

Other Graphic Organizers

Other graphic organizers also have been employed to capture cultural information about families (e.g., Thomlison, 2002). Such tools help to illuminate the powerful dynamics of cultural forces operating on the individual, family, or group.

In addition, visual tools have been used to focus on individual and family histories (e.g., Duhl, 1981); family structure, development, and problem solving (e.g., Meyerstein, 1979); gender role developmental histories (e.g., Green, 2003); recollections of one's family-of-origin (e.g., Coopersmith, 1980); individual and family self-perceptions (e.g., Thomlison, 2002); and sources of personal validation (e.g., Ivey, D'Andrea, Ivey, & Simek-Morgan, 2002). Such tools highlight individual and family contextual and temporal factors as these might affect issues promoting treatment.

All of these techniques are methods to pictorially represent the significant interpersonal and intrapsychic phenomena that help shape the ongoing experiences, interpretations, decisions, and actions of clients. Separately, these tools have proven their clinical utility. However, these graphic assessment devices do not explicitly address the issues of self-in-context or family-in-context and do not capture the larger contexts that influence human and systems development over time.

THE COMMUNITY GENOGRAM PERSPECTIVE: CAPTURING INDIVIDUAL, RELATIONAL, FAMILY, COMMUNITY, AND CULTURAL RELATIONSHIPS

The community genogram synthesizes many intra- and interpersonal factors in an organized and simple to use format. As an interactive assessment device, the community genogram captures holistically—in one representation—many of the variables targeted by other graphic assessment devices. Further, although other devices are predominantly used at the beginning of treatment for assessment and treatment-planning purposes, the community genogram can be referred to, modified, and enhanced throughout counseling and therapy. Because the community genogram is conceptually different from other graphic assessment methods, it is important to review the perspectives that led to its construction and use.

Historically, in northern European and U.S. cultures, individuals and families have tended to be viewed as isolated entities. Intrapsychic and intrafamilial dynamics were the primary focuses of counseling and therapy. Rarely were the interactions between clients and wider social contexts considered. Feminist theorists and therapists (see Goldner, 1993; Hare-Mustin, 1978; Luepnitz, 1988; Whipple, 1999; Williams & Wittig, 1997) raised the concern that classical theories of treatment, whether individually oriented or family focused, did not attend to the cultural factors that contributed to client distress.

Paralleling feminist critiques, multiculturalists also criticized traditional counseling models for the lack of respect shown to ethnic and racial sensitivities (see, Cheatham, 1990; D'Andrea & Daniels, 2001; Falicov, 1988; Hardy, 1990; Ibrahim, 1985; Pedersen, 1991). All clients, in traditional models of treatment, were treated the same, regardless of their age, cultural background, and gender. Today, clinicians recognize the need to provide culturally responsive treatment in a way that will not perpetuate oppression from wider social forces.

Individuals and families do not develop alone, as pawns of the environment. Nor do they develop independent of their external world. The community genogram is based on an ecosystemic perspective (Auerswald, 1983), which integrates individual and systems theories to consider the holistic development of clients. It is our opinion that the individual develops within a family, within a community setting, and within a societal and cultural milieu. Thus, it is the transaction between individual, family, and environment that is the dynamic force of development and adaptation (see Axelson, 1999; Harland, 1987; Ivey, Gonçalves, & Ivey, 1989; Vygotsky, 1934/1986).

According to Minuchin (1974), the family serves two basic functions: (1) to provide for the psychosocial needs of their members and (2) to balance the demands of the broader culture with their own needs and cultural mores. Similarly, we posit that families provide a primal socialization matrix for individuals to develop, and as individuals develop, the family's boundaries extend to include wider contexts that influence different aspects of each individual, each relationship, and the system as a whole. Simultaneously, families are also subsystems of larger social units, and, as such, they rely on their developmental and contextual histories to give meaning to and operate within larger social entities. Figure 1.1 demonstrates one ecosystemic method to conceptualize the mediating role of the family across time. The dynamics within and among the levels are conceptualized as four concentric circles specifying that cultural, societal, community, and family dynamics are operating within the relationship development of family members. The significant effects of these dynamics must be accounted for in a culturally responsive, non-oppressive approach to counseling and therapy. As demonstrated within the family system level of the diagram, each interacting individual carries

FIGURE 1.1. The Family as the Mediating Context for Human and Systemic Development

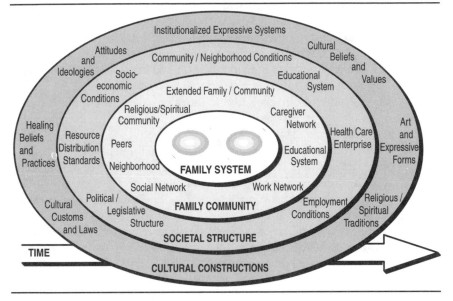

elements of all four levels as they naturally work to evolve personal meaning about themselves and others through the lens of the family context. For this reason, we consider the family system as the primary, but not exclusive, domain for the creation of the initial impressions of our sense of self and self-in-relation that we carry with us, to some extent, throughout our lives.

This holistic perspective permits clinicians and clients to access numerous sources of personal and collective strength that can be used to reevaluate the past and effect change in current life tasks and future adaptation. It can widen the analytic lens used by clinicians and clients so that they might perceive and target major stressors and strengths, not only as these are situated in individuals and families, but also as these are located in communities, prevailing cultural contexts, and the interactions that occur among all four domains. Personal, interpersonal, and interactive resources residing within these multiple contexts can be identified and marshaled to facilitate therapeutic growth.

Notice that the element of time is represented in Figure 1.1. Our understanding of self and self-in-relation evolves over time, through a cultural exchange process among individuals, families, significant others, and resonating community and cultural constructions. Sociohistorical conditions over time and across contexts inform the social structures for the exchange. Individual and family characteristics, developmental trajectories, and positions of power and influence within the structure all impact on the meaning-making process and contribute to human development within a specific time and place. For example, the abstract concepts of culture and society both inform individual and collective development and are influenced by the actions of individuals and groups. In this way the thread of cultural constructions and societal structures weaves through the array of unique individual and family differences; "it allows for a more or less easily negotiated sense of living in a shared world" (Wentworth & Wentworth, 1997, p. 42). The family is a primal matrix for individuals to learn about negotiating their shared world.

Appreciating this comprehensive view of human and systemic development requires that clinicians purposefully seek information about all four levels at different times. Unfortunately, our most common graphic device, the family genogram, may not always assist in this expanded assessment. The family genogram is very effective at highlighting the familial and genetic influences on individual and family functioning. Its historical emphasis expands the time frame so that clients can consider intergenerational patterns instead of assuming that all issues develop and end within their current family structure. This temporal perspective is one aspect of the client-in-relation. Missing, however, are influences and interactions that occurred outside the family. Work, school, church, community agencies, friends, neighbors, and prevailing sociocultural and political themes are not effectively integrated in the traditional family genogram.

Similarly, cultural influences, if not directly observable within the family domain, are usually overlooked in the traditional family genogram. The degree to which culture shapes issues such as decision-making preferences, interactional prescriptions, relational tendencies, and demonstrations of respect and affection might not surface in the analysis of family genograms. Further, if conflicts, differences, or power differentials exist between the family and the wider sociocultural context, these might be neglected due to the intense scrutiny paid to intrafamilial issues.

The community genogram can be a highly useful complement to the family genogram in that it additionally provides a look outside the family—at the interactions that occur between clients and their communities. The traditional three-generation family tree structure of the family genogram is not suitable to capture the wider interaction among clients, families, communities, and cultures. Within the community genogram approach, various types of family graphics become possible to clarify how individual, family, and the wider contexts contribute to and construe notions of self, self-in-relation, health, distress, and disorder. For example, what significant events, people, institutions, and prevailing themes in the wider community influence the current situation a client may be dealing with? In which relationships and settings does the client exert or acquiesce power? How does the external environment exercise privilege or oppression over the individual, family, and relational groups? To what degree does the client have the power to influence these external forces, now and in the future? How does the client interpret these interactions and how can the strengths inherent within and across these relationships be marshaled for therapeutic purposes?

The community genogram expands the vision of mental health services to not only capturing individual dynamics but also examining the relational dynamics within which clients operate. The community genogram can be used to identify key dimensions of client constructions relating to

- Self
- Self-in-relation
- Relational systems
- The wider sociocultural context
- Developmental history
- Contextual history
- Life tasks and functions

Further, attention can be given to the constructs most possible of serving the mental health needs of clients. Individuals, families, and wider social and cultural environments are seen as both unique structures of analysis and as interrelated components that make up the wider interactive system of human and systemic development.

The community genogram thus provides a vehicle for both culturally responsive and contextually sensitive assessment and treatment planning. As clients gradually learn to think of themselves as persons-in-context or systems-in-context, many more resources for positive development will begin to appear in the therapeutic environment. Blame and responsibility will tend to shift from either a predominant individual-focus or a predominant other-focus to a balance in which individual, family, community, and cultural attribution can be considered. We believe clinicians and clients will find this new balance of client and context helpful in defining a more positive reconceptualization of counseling and therapy. And it is fun and enables everyone's participation along the way.

Viewing Development in Context: Elizabeth

This case represents a straightforward approach to using community genograms with clients. Elizabeth (54) has recently retired from government service with the Air Force, for which she worked as a guidance counselor at military high schools. Elizabeth is a trained counseling professional and is focusing on beginning a second career as a self-employed trainer/educator, consultant, and counselor. She currently works at a university counseling center while she pursues her doctorate. We will use Elizabeth's graphics and analysis throughout the first four chapters.

Figure 1.2 shows a series of overlapping wheels that Elizabeth has chosen to represent her exploration of contextual influences across her life span. Each wheel represents a stage in life and each wheel drives the next one. The wheels vary in size depending on the amount of time spent in a particular stage. In the wheels she refers to a combination of influences including environmental (including other people), ancestral, biological/physical, spiritual, psychological, and social factors. At the hub of each wheel, Elizabeth placed an *I*. In referring to the *I* that represents herself, Elizabeth says, "I am as fluid in my development as the wheel, changing all the time—in relationship to others, the environment, and myself."

The spokes of a wheel depict themes and issues. Elizabeth believes that "all the major, meaningful or . . . impactful spokes in life's stages thread in some way throughout life. But some of them evolve into different presenting situations." The spokes of each wheel, then, "are positioned so that they weave their way through life's stages. Some spokes are thicker than others depending on their strength or prominence."

Elizabeth explains that the spokes or threads may be manifested in "games" and "scripts" that are played out in interactions. The spaces between the spokes are the "texture of life, the time spaces, the environment within which life is lived." The perimeters of the wheels are "the transition points to the next major life stage." The series of interlocking wheels encompasses multiple dimensions and is influenced by her ancestors as well as those in this physical plane, including a global community, extended family, and primary or birth family. In Elizabeth's words, "the idea is that life is a journey influenced by what comes before it, what is contained within it, and what surrounds it."

For Elizabeth, this depiction "captures the circular, ever-evolving image/nature of everything." Transformation or transcendence of major events or issues can occur through becoming aware of and understanding one's histories/games and scripts. Once games and scripts are understood, a person can rewrite them. "Some events influence or shape development more than others, and differing combinations of events or situations, coupled with various interventions that may take place, change the course of one's life, but we each remain at any point in time the composite of it all." We will resume Elizabeth's analysis in further chapters.

FIGURE 1.2. Elizabeth: A Life Span Perspective

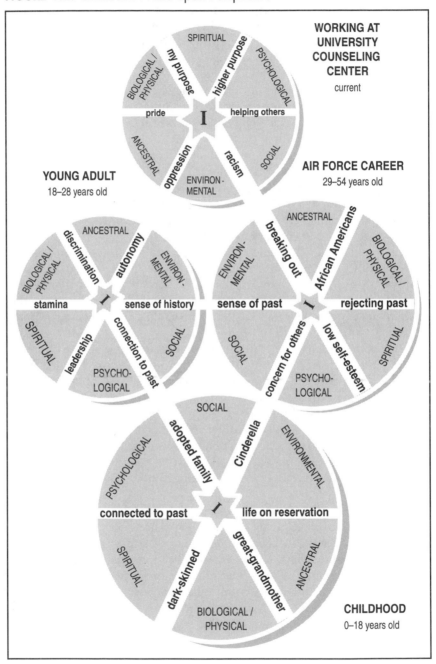

USING COMMUNITY GENOGRAMS THROUGHOUT
THE COUNSELING AND THERAPY PROCESS

Clients are actively engaged in the construction and interpretation of their community genograms. By asking clients to identify, represent, and articulate specific details of their lives, clinicians can hear the clients' own formulation of issues that led them to treatment. The client narratives also will indicate potential areas for change and success. The therapist can amplify hidden strengths, and client self-disclosure can generate new insights and ways to frame their realities. Reflections on old images, stories, and experiences can lead to a new view of self, family, and/or group. In short, the development of a community genogram can frequently move from an assessment and descriptive process to a significant strategy for change that remains available throughout counseling and therapy.

Community genograms are used to obtain awareness of clients' cultural legacies, important episodes in clients' contextual and developmental histories, and untapped potential resources for change. This clinical information provides a basis for practitioners to develop hypotheses about presenting issues that may be connected to community and cultural factors. Furthermore, community genograms directly enable clients to assume an active role in determining the focus and course of treatment. We will use the case of Alex to illustrate the application of the community genogram throughout all phases of the therapeutic process.

Alex (see Figure 1.3), a recently divorced mother of two, entered treatment with self-doubt, low self-esteem, and questions regarding her ability to be a good mother, friend, and worker. Upon completing an analysis of her community genogram, she noted both influential family-of-origin rules and external community and cultural forces that contributed to her depression. These rules and forces would become the predominant focus of treatment.

The Initial Phase of Therapy

Community genograms are used at every stage of the counseling and therapy process. In the initial phase, community genograms provide ways to involve clients in coconstructing the treatment focus. As a nonthreatening and enjoyable approach, community genograms help integrate a vast amount of intellectually and emotionally stimulating client information into a concise, usable framework that clients, clinicians, and supervisors can review and comment on. The community genogram provides numerous options to consider for treatment planning, many of which would not be identified

FIGURE 1.3. An Illustrative Community Genogram: The Case of Alex

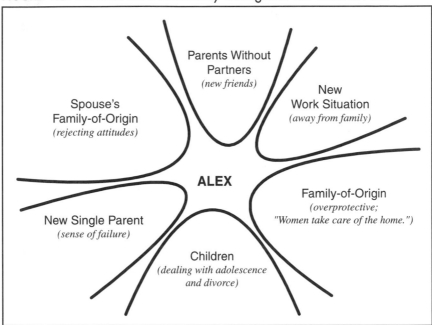

through a traditional psychosocial assessment or a standardized family genogram.

The therapeutic aim of community genogram work is to help clients include community and cultural factors in the formulation of and solution to their presenting issues. Viewing presenting issues in light of individual, family, and community dynamics helps clients normalize their experience. They begin to realize that their problems are not necessarily just their personal issues, but that problems are influenced by developmental histories, community concerns, and changing society. By exploring the dynamics depicted in their community genogram, clients can broaden their focus from self as the "identified patients" to the "interactions between clients and their environments."

> Alex's community genogram was used to raise her level of consciousness regarding what commonly occurs to recently divorced mothers in today's North American culture, if they learned and believed in traditional women's roles. For example, she came to realize that her gender role assumptions, similar to most middle-class Americans born

in the 1950s, would not hold up in her new situation. Her belief that "women take care of the home and family" and in turn "men financially take care of the home and family" would have to be reorganized, especially in light of contemporary legal and economic trends. She additionally could see that other adolescents, besides her daughter, exhibited similar school-related difficulties when transitioning through divorce. She also noted that her own family's overprotective nature and the cold, rejecting attitudes of her ex-in-laws were unfortunately common. By "normalizing" her situation, Alex could externalize the issues that prompted treatment. She was able to see her reactions as a natural and logical consequence from her developmental history and her current situational context.

Progress in Therapy: The Re-storying Process

Progress through therapy can be monitored by referring back to the community genogram and updating it as new information and interpretations become available. Counseling has been defined as the ability to help clients re-story their lives (Anderson & Goolishian, 1988; De Shazer, 1991; Gergen, 1999; Kittredge, 1999; Morgan, 2000; Polkinghorne, 1994; White & Epston, 1990). The community genogram offers visual illustrations that can generate and solidify modifications that are a result of the therapeutic encounter. Many clinicians use the community genogram as a concrete visualization of the progress made in treatment.

Often clients bring in new images and stories as they probe their issues and possible solutions. These new images are added to the community genogram to begin forming a tapestry of the client's life. Sometimes, new situation-specific or theme-specific community genograms are suggested to help clients deeply probe a particular time or life pattern. These specially focused community genograms bring out the nuances of the initial community genogram and stimulate opportunities for the re-storying process.

By "depathologizing" her depression and by noting her actual fortitude in the face of adversity, Alex could rejoin her community. Further, she could seek out resources available to her such as Parents Without Partners and recreational programs for children that included support groups for adolescents transitioning through divorce.

In Parents Without Partners, Alex met people who accepted her new role and shared their similar stories and their unique roads to success. Alex regained and generalized her positive identity as a single mother and woman who needed—and deserved—contextual accommodations from mainstream America to maintain a quality life for her and her family. Her composite community genogram depicts the new influence of this group and the lesser influence of those who did not accept her divorce. It identified strengths where there were negatives to begin. For example, her children were now considered assets and she felt more confident in her role as a single parent. In fact, she and three other employees successfully petitioned their employer to arrange for flex scheduling to accommodate to family circumstances.

Termination of Therapy

Using the community genogram as a terminating activity has been well received by both clinicians and clients. For clients, it provides a concrete point of reference to discuss the signs of their progress. They are able to see how they have reworked their initial impression of their presenting issues. Clients leave treatment feeling good about the changes that were initiated because of their analysis of the community genogram. Former problems have often been re-storied as strengths and assets. They also have learned new skills regarding how to broaden their lens when defining problematic issues, and thus can see multiple options for change.

For clinicians, the graphic illustrations are a visual record of treatment. Helping clients realize how they coconstructed their new stories and how they opened up new resources are essential components of the termination process. The tapestry of community genograms provides clients specific maps for the continuation of these therapeutic gains. The new stories and new resources are readily available in the community genograms and are used for discussion purposes at the end of therapy. Finally, the gift of community genograms at the end of treatment signifies the passing on, from clinician to client, a proven map that can be accessed in the future to make meaningful changes when necessary.

Alex entered treatment believing she was dealing with a depression that originated from her own weaknesses. Through her community genogram analysis, she recognized this symptom to represent years of living by traditional rules that were now outdated due to her circumstances and to external forces that did not accommodate to her and her family's needs. With this new outlook, she joined others who shared similar beliefs and knew roads to success that she could model. Treatment ended at the time Alex was referred to a lawyer who specialized in the economic necessities of single parents and in legally rebalancing child support issues.

CONCLUSION: THE MAP IS NOT THE TERRAIN

For illustrative purposes we use a variety of case scenarios throughout this book. The inferences, hypotheses, and treatment decisions generated from the case material do not necessarily represent the only path to follow. Just as each client-clinician relationship is truly unique and generates a particular coconstructed process, the material presented here simply represents our work with clients and is not intended to be the model treatment for other clients exhibiting similar symptoms.

Community genograms are in a sense secondhand information, representing the recollections and interpretations of our clients from original situations and interactions. We should therefore keep in mind the natural ability of individuals and families to minimize certain aspects and maximize other aspects of any recalled situation. However, because we are not historians but mental health professionals, our concern does not necessarily center on accuracy and verifiability. Rather, we often attempt to discern how deeply our clients are influenced by their interpretations. The community genogram is a way of focusing our therapeutic conversations and can go wherever our clients and we codetermine.

Although the community genogram is a subjective representation of experience, it does allow the systematic exploration of issues and themes that arise from the coconstruction and analytic process. It provides a continuous map to chart progress and to identify areas requiring further analysis. It is an invaluable tool to assist clients to re-story their lives so that they can maximize the strengths and positive resources they have available within themselves, their families, and their wider communities.

CHAPTER 2

How to Construct and Interpret Community Genograms: Exploring Self-in-Relation and Family-in-Relation

Community genograms are as personal as each individual who constructs them. To do this well, in a fashion that respects the unique qualities and expressive abilities of each client, a counselor much use nuanced professional knowledge and judgment. To accomplish this, the basic components of how to use community genograms will be the focus of this chapter. Counselors must understand the primary concepts that are captured by the community genogram before they can be expertly used in the treatment setting. The theoretical assumptions associated with the community genograms provide a framework to help professionals best adapt their use to the individual needs and learning styles of our clientele. There are five specific objectives in this chapter:

- **To provide a basic understanding of the concepts self-in-relation and family-in-relation**
- **To distinguish between separate and relational perspectives**
- **To consider how the dimension of power influences perspectives of the self**
- **To present the key assumptions undergirding the construction and interpretation of community genograms**
- **To provide the basic steps to constructing community genograms**

CLARIFYING VARIOUS DEFINITIONS OF SELF AND FAMILY

Answers to seemingly simple questions can be quite revealing. "Can you tell me about yourself?" "How would you define your family?" "How have your family and your community affected your life?" The focus of these questions—the multiple layers of individual identity and family identity—are at the heart of this book. The way clinicians ask their questions often deter-

16

mines how their clients think about their issues. Basically, our questions and conversational styles frame treatment.

The goal of this chapter is to provide specific therapeutic strategies to help generate and organize the multifaceted perspectives individuals and families carry with them concerning their sense of identity. The community genogram approach provides graphing tools and questioning strategies to explore the various ways clients view themselves over time and in different situations.

The concept of self is a twentieth-century phenomenon. Terms such as *individual* and *ego* were added to the psychological lexicon at the beginning of the 1900s and were popularized in the second half of this century. Statements like "Do your own thing," "Find my own space," "Looking for one-self," and "WII-FM—What's in it for me?" epitomized the psychological perspective of the "me-first" generation. Prior to that time, the concept of self was indistinguishable from the family and the community within which one developed.

The traditional individual counseling and therapy orientations (i.e., humanistic-experiential, psychodynamic, behavioral), which dominated the mental health field during most of the twentieth century, perpetuated a myth of individuals as detached from their surroundings (Hayes, 1994; Paniagua, 2001; Pedersen, 2000; Rigazio-DiGilio, Gonçalves, & Ivey, 1996). The primary focus of therapy was to treat the supposed pathology that resided within individuals. The field is currently seeking to recapture the importance of our personal linkages with the wider sociocultural environment. To differentiate the concept of an isolated self from a connected self, we use the term *self-in-relation*.

Similarly, the notion of the self-contained nuclear family was not widely accepted until the post–World War II era. Prior to that time, extended families, villages, and ethnic communities were the more familiar characteristics used to define the family. Popular television shows of the 1950s, such as *Leave It to Beaver*, *Ozzie and Harriet*, and *Father Knows Best*, epitomized the ideal family structure (i.e., 2 parents with 2.3 children) as primarily isolated from extended family and community.

In the 1960s and 1970s traditional theories of family therapy enlarged the treatment of so-called pathology to include an identified patient as well as members of her or his family. However, these theories still reinforced the notion of a family isolated from the wider context (D'Andrea & Daniels, 2001; Rigazio-DiGilio, 1997). We use the term *family-in-relation* to underscore the current trend to consider factors in the broader community and culture that have influenced family growth, development, and adaptation.

In this book, the terms *self-identity* and *collective identity* refer to the self-contained notions of the individual and family, respectively. On the other hand, the terms *self-in-relation* and *family-in-relation* communicate the transactive nature of self and family within the wider sociopolitical, community, and cultural environments. In this chapter, we explore the differences between these concepts by inviting you to respond to some questions about yourself and your family, both as separate entities and relational entities. The chapter includes some exercises that help you directly experience how individual, family, community, and cultural factors influence your sense of self-identity and self-in-relation.

DEFINING SELF, FAMILY, AND THE COMMUNITY: PRACTICE QUESTIONS

In order to personalize the meaning of self-identity and collective identity, we ask that you take a few moments to respond to some key questions. Feel free to write what immediately comes to your mind.

1. Focus on yourself for a moment. What occurs for you when you think about yourself?

Review your answer. How does family, community, or cultural influences factor into your sense of self-identity? Often people consciously or unconsciously use their identified cultural background as they reply to this question. By doing so, their answers are influenced by the values, norms, and rules of their community and cultural background. For example, individuals in the United States who respond to the statement "Tell me about yourself," often identify themselves by their vocational status: "I am a student, a therapist, or a teacher." In Norway, individuals frequently provide information about their family lineage: "I am the daughter of Jon and Gerta Andersen." In Italy, individuals might identify the town or region in which they were born: "I am Calabrese."

These same cultural factors also become evident when we explore who we are in relation to our family-of-origin; that is, how does our family background influence how we define ourselves?

2. Focus on your family-of-origin for a moment. What occurs for you when you focus on yourself in relation to your family-of-origin?

Review your two responses thus far. How did your self-identity change when you were asked to focus on your family-of-origin? Viewing ourselves through the eyes of our family often adds a new dimension to our sense of self-identity.

3. How does your family-of-origin define itself?

In this question, how did you determine the way your family-of-origin would define itself? That is, how did you define your family's collective identity? By considering our family as one entity we can see the common factors that influence all members of our household.

In terms of cultural influences, individuals from Western cultures often focus on their nuclear family in their responses: "I lived with my mom, dad, and four brothers." Extended family networks are referred to frequently by individuals from Mediterranean cultures: "When I married my wife, I really married her whole family." Broader definitions, including information about villages and tribal affiliations, might be included in responses from Africans and Native Americans: "I lived with my parents and siblings in a large family village," or "My family is Navajo."

Cultural influences also affect how we collectively define ourselves as families. Families from Western cultures tend to use societal standards to generate responses. "We are a middle-class family where both parents work and the children attend school." Asian families may focus on issues of legacy and closeness that tend to be influenced by definitions carried over from their elders: "We have always been a close-knit family and we will maintain this closeness no matter where we live."

Self-identities and collective identities also vary within cultures. It is not surprising that two males, close in age and born and raised in the same family, would respond differently to each question you have answered thus far, depending on their biological makeup, experiential backgrounds, interests, significant relationships, and positions in their family and other meaningful groups. It goes without saying, then, that responses from two persons, born and raised within the same community, but not related by blood, would vary even more. For example, a firstborn, privileged Iranian male living in Tehran would have a very different perception of self-identity and collective identity than a third-born Iranian female living within a farming community on the outskirts of the same city. Similarly, a first-generation Russian American family living in a predominantly Greek American community and raising young children would have a very different collective identity than a similar family, in a similar community, but raising adolescents. It is evident that within-culture differences are just as important as cross-cultural differences when understanding how individuals and families define themselves.

Learning why individuals or families use particular descriptors when responding to such questions can provide insight into how they perceive themselves, their relationships with others, and the nature of their life tasks. How individuals and families understand their own sense of identity helps to determine the beliefs and values they use as filters to experience, interpret, and adapt to everyday interactions in the world. Our identities and our belief systems influence the way we define success or failure, how to live a productive life, and what makes a relationship work.

Beyond family influences, our wider community also affects our sense of self-identity and our family's collective identity. For example, interactions with social groups and community institutions directly influence how we view our families and ourselves. If a person is attending a meeting of Alcoholics Anonymous, the phrase following his name usually identifies him as an alcoholic: "My name is Eric, and I am an alcoholic." On college campuses, it is not unusual for persons to define themselves by their educational status: "I am a senior, majoring in history." Irish Americans often refer to their religious affiliation: "We live in St. Joseph's parish."

In terms of families, consider two sets of parents who attend a parent-teacher conference to discuss the acting-out behavior of their child. The parents with a grasp of the political themes within the local educational community might define themselves as a family who must stand up for the rights of their child in an overpopulated school system. However, the parents without this understanding might define themselves, consciously or unconsciously, as somehow dysfunctional or inadequate. Individuals and families inhabiting communities experiencing civil stability and economic growth will develop very different self-identities and collective identities than individuals and families living in communities struggling with the stress of financial, social, or natural calamities. Consider the impact that the events of September 11, 2001, have had on our individual and collective identities.

4. Reflect on your community-of-origin for a moment, that is, the community that primarily influenced you. What happens for you when you focus on yourself in relation to this community?

How did your self-identity change when you were asked to think more broadly about the community influences? What community factors figured prominently in your responses? How did the local geography or the social, religious, and community groups with which you were affiliated influence you? What economic and political conditions pervaded your neighborhood? Answers to questions such as these help us to understand the nature and influence of the wider community on our sense of self-identity.

It should be noted that larger groups, such as peer, vocational, spiritual, civic, and recreational networks, also influence our development. These larger networks bind people together through a commitment to shared visions and common purposes. In your response, you might have highlighted certain community qualities or symbols, such as accomplishments, history, values, heroes and heroines, community status, expectations, and within-group differences: "I belong to a civic-minded group that wanted to educate our community's children about AIDS." "We were part of a larger group of immigrants looking for economic opportunities." "Some of those in our church believe in pro-choice, while others are strictly pro-life, and this has caused a rift in the community." "Our basketball team won the state finals." These responses about community influences on your sense of self-identity are just as expansive, diverse, and telling as the information gleaned from questions focused solely on individual and family attributes.

5. How would your family-of-origin define itself in relation to this same community?

How did you determine the way your family-of-origin, as a collective unit, might define itself in relation to this community? Your response might have been governed by the degree to which your family shared common expectations with this wider community. For example, families who reflect the community's ideals about family values, civic mindedness, and spirituality would have a very different collective identity than families whose beliefs and behaviors are at odds with the general norms: "Because we were seen as outsiders in a very tight-knit community, we could pull together as a family." "When we moved to a more prestigious community, we got caught up in conspicuous consumption. It took us a while to see how much this affected our family relationships and our spirituality." Our family's relationship to the wider community has direct influence on both our sense of self-identity and our sense of collective identity.

Surfacing Elements of Self-in-Relation and Family-in-Relation

Your responses to the questions listed thus far also indicate how you define yourself in relation to the significant persons and events in your life. Your responses suggest the ways you have constructed your self-identity and your family's collective identity throughout the social interactions you have been involved with over time.

Look at your answers to Question 1. How many of the descriptors represent who you are in relationship to others? For example, words such as *brother*, *daughter*, *helper*, *student*, and *spouse* all imply your role within a relationship. Even some individualistic characteristics you may have listed, such as *successful*, *happy*, or *sensitive*, reflect ways you have come to understand or experience yourself because of your interactions with primary relationships or in specific situations.

Consider the significant influences you thought about as you responded to the question referring to yourself and your family-of-origin (Question 2). For example, did you think about persons such as a favorite aunt, a critical parent, an overindulging grandparent, or a supportive adult who is the live-in companion of your father? Did specific events such as the illness and death of a parent, the birth of a sibling, a divorce, or a family move show up in your response?

And now consider the significant influences you thought about when you responded to questions about yourself and your primary community (Question 4). For example, were you drawn to think about significant persons, such as a favorite minister or a critical teacher; significant institutions, such as your church or your community recreation center; significant places such as adolescent hangouts or favorite community or neighborhood gathering spots; or significant events, such as a community flood, a riot, or a winning athletic team?

What is emerging through this reflective analysis is a more complex notion of how your self-identity has been influenced by your interactions with particular people and in particular environments. We label this more interactive definition of the *self* as the *self-in-relation* or the *self-in-context*.

Your family can also be viewed from this interactive perspective. Consider your answers to Questions 3 and 5. Can you identify the broader influences that fashioned your perception of your family's sense of *family-in-relation* or *family-in-context*, when you responded to these questions? What persons, groups, institutions, places, and events shaped the sense of family-in-relation?

Thus far we have been exploring the difference between a perspective that isolates and draws a strong boundary around the individual or the family system and a more interactive perspective that widens the lens to consider self-family-community-cultural connections in a more holistic fashion. The basic assumption is that the self-identities used by individuals and the collective identities used by families are formed and internalized through influential social transactions.

A BROAD VIEW OF EXTENDED FAMILY: ELIZABETH

When referring back to her community genogram, Elizabeth noted that her sense of self-in-relation is much stronger than her sense of self-as-individual. She added *we* to each of the hubs. As she states, "the *we* in me is significantly more prominent than and indeed shapes the *I*." Using Elizabeth's childhood years (see Figure 2.1), she explored issues of her family-of-origin.

Extended family has been central to Elizabeth's "healthy psychological growth and development since birth." Elizabeth's idea of family takes a much

FIGURE 2.1. Elizabeth: A Childhood Wheel

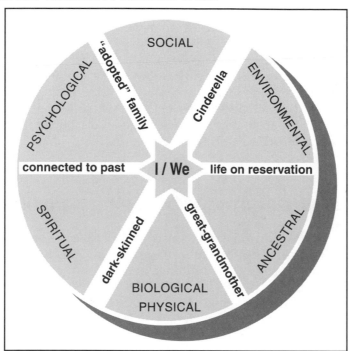

broader view than the one held in our dominant U.S. culture. For Elizabeth, extended family is not simply limited to those relationships in which one is related by blood, but is more related to the spirit. Extended family relationships are those that are experienced as mutually intimate, nurturing, accepting, supportive, enduring, and having a sense of connectedness. Relationships with persons outside the nuclear family can take on the role of parent, sibling, or child. For example, a female friend can become a "sister," and older, caring neighbors can become "parents." Individuals can be adopted by others at any age.

Elizabeth explains that this sense of family reflects beliefs of Native Americans in which there are formal ceremonies in which a person can be adopted into a clan. Elizabeth, for example, who is a member of the Delaware Nation but does not know any of her people, was adopted as a "sister" by a member of the Muskogee Creek Wind Clan, giving her a sense of belonging until and if she is able to locate her own people. Should she desire to do so, she can become an adoptive member of this woman's clan in an official ceremony.

For Elizabeth, this view of family "opens up a whole different perspective and understanding about other planes in life, about ancestors, and their alive nature within our lives, about the connectiveness of all people and the true 'family of mankind.'" In this way, people have the ability to "enter into all sorts of different relationships." This perspective has been a wonderful resource for Elizabeth throughout her life. She is able to have strong, deep, interdependent, and enduring connections with others. Through these relationships much is shared: nurturance, support, understanding, love, acceptance, celebrations, and disappointments. Extended family has provided and continues to provide a profound richness in Elizabeth's life.

THE SEPARATE ENTITY–RELATIONAL ENTITY CONTINUUM

Now take a comprehensive look at the answers to all the questions you have responded to thus far. Is it difficult for you to get an idea of where your self-identity ends and your sense of self-in-relation begins, or can you readily distinguish between the two? Additionally, are you able to separate your collective identity from your sense of family-in-relation, or is the boundary between the two unclear? Although these are two extreme ends of a broad continuum—from separate entities to relational entities—where we position our families and ourselves on this continuum is influenced by several different factors. Two key factors seem particularly relevant: boundaries and perceived sense of power and influence.

Boundaries

One key factor has to do with the degree to which individuals and families are aware of the varying amounts of overlap between themselves as separate entities and themselves as relational entities. For example, a white middle-class Irish American male with a strong and rigid sense of himself as a separate entity might interpret being passed over for a promotion by an equally qualified, African American female as a reflection of his own incompetence. A similar male, with a strong and rigid sense of himself as a relational entity might interpret this decision as a consequence of reverse discrimination. A male positioned on the continuum in a more balanced and flexible fashion could review the situation-in-context. Issues about his suitability for the responsibilities inherent in the promotion, the institution's ethical imperative toward affirmative action promotion policies, the qualifications of the successful applicant, and the interactions that occurred during the interview process would all be considered. Being balanced affords the opportunity to evaluate each situation on its own—given a specific set of factors—and not automatically jump to a global response of either "I must be at fault or responsible" or "The system must be at fault or responsible."

Some families, on the surface, tend to emphasize an individualistic mentality that elevates concepts of the self and the nuclear family. For example, many families operating within a corporate American societal frame tend to fall into this category. The only way the recent atrocities in the business world, such as the alleged financial duplicity at Enron, World Com, and Tyco, could be carried out by so many people in high levels of their organization is by limiting their sense of connectedness to others and viewing personal economic advancement as omnipotent.

Other families may tend to place more emphasis on themselves as relational entities and may not draw the same clear distinctions between self, family, community, and culture. For example, many families functioning in African, Native American, Asian, and European cultures share a wider view of family. Just as with individuals, the rigidity of the boundary families place around themselves will determine if they can flexibly respond to different circumstances and challenges.

Power and Influence: More Practice Questions

The second key factor encompasses the actual or perceived power arrangements that exist in our significant affiliations and the actual or perceived resources we have to affect these power arrangements. The definitions that we construct regarding self-in-relation and family-in-relation are partially based on the degree of influence we believe we have in any given situation, role, or context. Let's begin with some personal examples.

1. Name a time and/or relationship where you felt powerless and unable to control what was happening. What were your feelings and thoughts? Who or what held the most influence and how were power and resources wielded to help or hurt?
2. What is a relationship you feel you had the power and resource to influence? What are your current feelings and thoughts about yourself in this relationship?

Power differentials and available resources are not constant phenomena. These change over time and within different contexts, and in so doing, change the degree of perceived or actual influence. For example, influential families or families considered normal in today's society are not the same families who exercised power or were perceived as normal in prevailing societies of the 1950s. Teachers may appear in charge within their own classrooms but exercise different degrees of influence in parent-teacher conferences or with other teachers and supervisors.

Individuals and families may exercise different degrees of influence in their interpersonal, intrafamilial, and intracommunity relations. College students are often quite active and influential within their peer group but frequently relinquish some of their power when they return to their parents' home. Some individuals can be very influential at work but withdraw from leadership positions in their church or community organizations or vice versa.

The degree of perceived influence, either exercised or received, in any relationship impacts the position that one takes on the separate entities–relational entities continuum. In this regard, power and resources are noticeable links that connect us to others.

For example, in some unbalanced power situations, when people are placed in disempowering contexts and choose not to exercise influence by using available resources, the ties that bind can be held very loosely. There are many ways clients use the behaviors associated with learned helplessness (Seligman, 1975) to minimize personal responsibility for the choices they make, either explicitly or tacitly. It is easy, in these circumstances, to draw a strong boundary around the self and disconnect from the other. In other unbalanced power situations, however, when people are disempowered and do not have the resources to exercise influence, the ties that bind can be held very tightly. Examples of this include genocide, economic and political oppression, institutional racism, and gender bias. It is much harder, in these circumstances, for the disempowered persons to draw a strong boundary around the self and disconnect from the other, as the "other" may indeed have the power and resources to invade and affect the environments and well-being of the disempowered.

When we are empowered and choose to engage in a decision-making process where we use our resources to create unbalanced power situations, we may choose to create a context where there are either impenetrable or invasive boundaries between the self and the other, thereby relying on a separate sense of self. Conversely, when we are empowered and choose to engage in decision-making processes where we use our resources to create balanced or liberating situations, our sense of responsibility for the other is heightened and the boundaries between our environments and well-being and those of the other become more permeable.

Illustrating the Continuum

Both boundaries and degree of power and influence affect the ways individuals and families construct a sense of themselves-in-relation. To further elaborate the key factors that affect our evolving sense of self, family, self-in-relation, and family-in-relation, let us consider an immigrant family living in an ethnic community within an urban setting where the majority of the city population and teaching faculty are white.

In many schools, if a child refuses to attend school, the first response by the professionals is to blame the child and then the family. Less frequently would the educational and mental health personnel attempt to analyze how the school system itself and/or the community could be influencing the child's and the family's behavior.

The family that can balance a sense of itself as a separate entity and a relational entity might be able to frame their child's behavior as, in part, a legitimate response to a devaluing and dehumanizing learning situation. This family and, in turn, their child, may develop a sense of self-in-relation and family-in-relation that more accurately reflects the oppressive factors inherent in their wider community.

On the other hand, the family that perceives itself as a separate entity may be unable to see the influence of the wider environment and may absorb the school system and community's labels of deviance and incompetence into their sense of their child and themselves-in-relation.

Additionally, while the "balanced" family may be able to understand the partial legitimacy of their child's response, if they do not have access to available resources in the community, then their inability to affect broader change could soon have a demoralizing effect. However, with available resources, they may take actions to change the situation. For example, they could work to develop a community charter school dedicated to meeting the educational needs of all children within a culturally sensitive fashion. Their action would be the result of a more positive sense of self-in-relation and family-in-relation.

Knowing how individuals and families come to construct their own identities and their identities in relation to others is important to the counseling and therapy process. Additionally, knowing the degree to which individuals and families understand, are affected by, and can influence the interrelationship between individuals, families, and communities widens the conceptual lens we use in therapy. Finally, by understanding how individuals and families use boundaries and degrees of influence to construct their sense of self helps clinicians determine effective points of intervention and culturally responsive therapeutic strategies. The community genogram is an interactive tool that can be used to help clients organize and explore issues of boundaries and power as they relate to their own definitions of self-in-relation and family-in-relation.

CONSTRUCTING THE COMMUNITY GENOGRAM

"It takes a village to raise a child." This well-known African proverb scores the importance of the community genogram. Our original community or "village" is where we learn the culture that will remain with us through our lifetime. Communities consist of our family and perhaps extended family; friends and neighbors; schools; work settings; the physical geography of the community territory; church or spiritual connections; and other unique factors. Our personal experiences within our communities are as unique as our fingerprints.

Cultures, communities, villages, families, groups, and individuals are all interconnected. Difficulty or trauma in the community, such as a tornado, a mass shooting, or the loss of jobs through the closure of a manufacturing plant, deeply affect not only individual lives, but also what occurs in the family and various community groups. In effect, one major community event can change the total culture. In turn, the madness or skill of one individual can affect the total system. Witness what occurs when a criminal terrorizes a neighborhood, such as the snipers in the Washington, DC, area and near Columbus, OH, or what occurs with the positive impact of a single individual such as Martin Luther King.

The community genogram is a way to introduce a positive, strength-oriented view of self and family into the therapy and counseling process—showing how we are all selves-in-relation or families-in-relation one to another. The community genogram is also a way to discover the important groups (e.g., churches, schools, peer groups, neighborhoods) that influence who we are as individuals and collective family systems. If we take a life span perspective, we can become aware that the nature of community changes and expands as we grow. The center for most children is the family, commonly followed by peer groups for many teens, work groups for many adults, and the family again for many elders.

Many individual and family problems and concerns are related to community, especially when we consider family as central to that community. The community genogram, while focusing on personal, family, and group strengths, also provides an opportunity to understand the context of our clients' past or current issues.

Key Assumptions Related to Community Genograms

There are several important assumptions related to the use of community genograms:

- Clients are viewed, not as separate individuals and families, but as entities who are integrally and reciprocally connected within a person/family/community/cultural relationship.
- All individuals and families hold beliefs about their own separate identities and their sense of self-in-relation and family-in-relation.

- Significant people, situations, and events within communities influence a client's current view of self and self-in-relation, and family, and family-in-relation.
- The degree of congruence between clients' thoughts, behaviors, and feelings, and those of the prevailing community and culture will help determine the sense of self-in-relation and family-in-relation that clients exhibit.
- The degree of influence, exerted or received, will help determine the sense of self-in-relation and family-in-relation that clients exhibit.
- Community genograms can be used to search for dynamics that are a result of self-in-relation and family-in-relation issues.
- Community genograms can be used to identify potential sources of strength within individuals, families, communities, and prevailing cultural themes to facilitate change.
- Community genogram methods emphasize a coconstructive relationship between therapist and client.
- Community genograms can document the progress of treatment.

The Basic Components: The Case of Rita

Community genograms graphically represent significant relationships, events, and situations that have come to shape clients' experiences over time. There are basic elements and questioning strategies that can be used to draw out this information. These are defined and illustrated in Chapters 3 and 4. These components include graphic ways to depict the degree of closeness, congruity, and influence that exist between clients and the particular persons and relationships, prevailing community and cultural themes, and predominant events and institutions within which clients live. These components also include questioning strategies that facilitate a broader lens through which issues are defined and resources located.

The community genogram in Figure 2.2, for example, visually represents the intrafamilial and external community influences affecting the sadness and lethargy of a 68-year-old Polish American female experiencing a major depressive episode. After years of raising her three children and witnessing the death of her husband of 42 years, Rita has reluctantly agreed to relocate to an assisted-living facility. Rita acknowledges that her frequent thoughts of suicide can only be monitored in a more secure residence, but she is still resentful about the move.

In coconstructing a current representation of her situation, Rita identified five critical factors that were either positively or negatively impinging upon her sense of connectedness to others and her sense of well-being. These form the white space intruding on the center of the diagram and include her financial difficulties, physical impairment, family's traditions and ways of acting with one another, religious beliefs, and new living situation.

FIGURE 2.2. An Illustrative Community Genogram: The Case of Rita

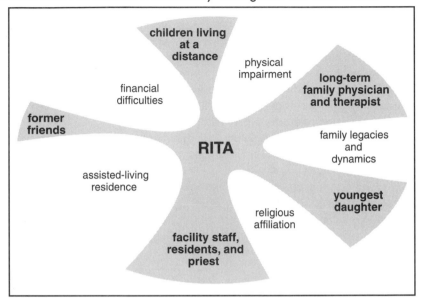

In conversation with her therapist, Rita discussed her disappointment regarding her lack of contact with her old friends and the difficulties making friends at the new facility. However, Rita also was able to identify her newly forming affiliations with the resident staff and priest; her continuing bond with her family, particularly with her youngest daughter; the love she feels from her former friends and family physician; and her trusting relationship with her therapist of 3 years. The shaded areas in Figure 2.2 represent these connections.

Using the community genogram analysis, notice how the boundaries of three critical factors (i.e., assisted-living residence, financial situation, and physical impairment) close off Rita's connectedness to two significant groups (former friends and family). Using this aspect of the visual picture, Rita could understand that social connections, her psychological issues, and family traditions and dynamics influenced her lack of connectedness to her new community. Now notice how the pathways connecting Rita to her other three primary relationships (i.e., long-term physician and therapist, youngest daughter, and facility staff, residents, and priest) are more open due to the influence of the three critical areas noted on her community genogram (i.e., assisted-living residence and therapist, religious affiliation, and family lega-cies and dynamics). Focusing on this aspect of the visual representation, Rita could explore with the therapist how her new residence, her religious con-victions, and the same family traditions and dynamics fostered continued and newly forming relationships with the resident staff and helped her feel good about herself. Rita became more aware of the comfort and security provided to her by her new relationships at the assisted-living facility, religious beliefs and values, and the strong sense of family connectedness she experienced. Finally, Rita was able to wonder how to use her resources (i.e., family tradi-tions, religious affiliations, new comfort in living residence) to find alterna-tive ways to reconnect with her old friends.

The Flexible Nature of the Community Genogram

The community genogram is more of a concept than a static tool. It has to be flexible to capture the wide range of community data clients may present. It has to be malleable enough to illustrate subtleties that clients may wish to explore. Because of these issues, a variety of visual models and questioning strategies can be used to coconstruct community genograms. Once the basic components of the community genogram are learned and practiced, clini-cians can use these as a flexible blueprint, adding their own creativity, and tailoring the format and questions to meet the needs, learning styles, and creativities of their clients.

Rather than fixing on a single visual framework for a community geno-gram, Ivey (1995) suggests that you work with clients to develop their own models. Many clients like to draw literal maps of their communities with pictures of their families, schools, and churches drawn in.

Using computer-generated clip art, Figure 2.3 depicts the memories of a daughter of the Gesili family, a second-generation Italian American family who resided in a community-of-origin that was a mixture of Italian and Irish ethnic groups. The Irish community first inhabited the neighborhood, fac-ing discrimination in religious, educational, and employment arenas. After many years, they were in charge of these primary institutions. When the Ital-ians came to live in the neighborhood's lower status housing, the Irish com-munity treated them as they themselves had been treated. The businesses and the better housing were closed to Italians. NINA signs previously used as a barrier for Irish employment (No Irish Need Apply) were now used to keep Italian immigrants from entering the work force. This family felt the privi-lege of living in their own Italian community, as well as the oppression of the Irish community. A fond memory entailed family-initiated annual block parties, as, increasingly, both neighborhoods came together in this family's

FIGURE 2.3. A Computer-Generated Visual Map: The Case of the Gesili Family

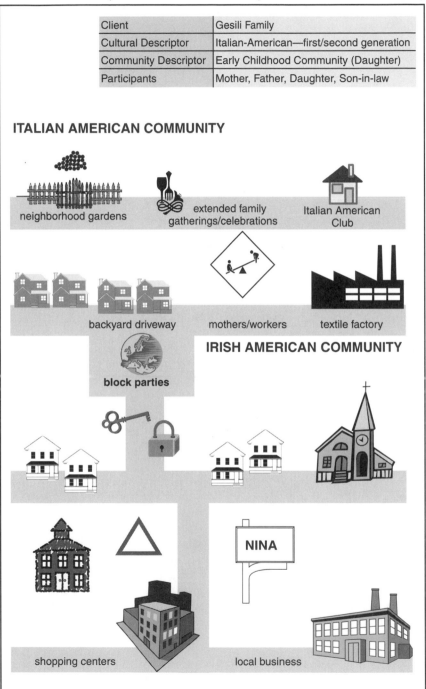

Client	Gesili Family
Cultural Descriptor	Italian-American—first/second generation
Community Descriptor	Early Childhood Community (Daughter)
Participants	Mother, Father, Daughter, Son-in-law

ITALIAN AMERICAN COMMUNITY

neighborhood gardens

extended family gatherings/celebrations

Italian American Club

backyard driveway

mothers/workers

textile factory

block parties

IRISH AMERICAN COMMUNITY

NINA

shopping centers

local business

backyard. The block parties became the key for unlocking eventual integration of these two communities.

Another positive recollection recounted how upon gaining citizenship, the maternal grandmother worked in a vanilla extract factory where the women would take turns watching their children throughout the day. Each woman took a different break time to be outside with the children. The group of children began life-long friends integrating both Italian and Irish families. This visual map assisted the Gesilis in realizing that there were many sources of strength and resiliency sprinkled throughout their neighborhood. (Authors' note: members of the Gesili family participated in a series of interviews to illustrate the use of computer-generated images as memory anchors to pull together the wider contextual backdrop in which individuals and families form their sense of self and self-in-relation.)

Notice that the coding box at the top right of the figure records pertinent client information and is helpful in organizing this visual information. The coding box identifies the client, the cultural and community descriptors, and the participants. The daughter was the person who created this visual map and she is noted in parentheses.

Another useful visual model is that of the relational community genogram (see Figure 2.4). Robert and Dorothy sought treatment after many years of dealing with Robert's cancer. They both reported feeling increased stress and less mutual support. The couple was introduced to the relational diagram as a tool to represent their common and individual perceptions of the situation. The therapist asked them each to identify those significant others they were interacting with at the moment. These groups and individuals were placed in such a way as to form a circle around each individual and are in bold print. Common groups, such as their children, each other ("partner"), and professionals and friends at the medical facility, were placed in the center of the relational diagram. This common area is highlighted in Figure 2.4 with the gray background. Groups and individuals that were not common were placed on the exterior sides of each individual. The therapist solicited meaningful activities and aspects of their lives, such as religious life, occupational issues, neighborhood and community relations. Common aspects including family, home, and cancer treatment were again placed in the middle between them.

Next, the therapist asked them to discuss the nature of their relationship with their significant others. Robert explained that he really enjoys his "patient colleagues" and has been relying on them since the original diagnosis. He said the other person, besides Dorothy, with whom he confides is his rabbi. He didn't spend much time with the others. The closed gaps between Robert and such groups as children, extended family, and professional colleagues represent his lack of interaction with these groups. On the other hand, the wide-open access

FIGURE 2.4. An Illustrative Relational Community Genogram: The Case of Dorothy and Robert Feldman

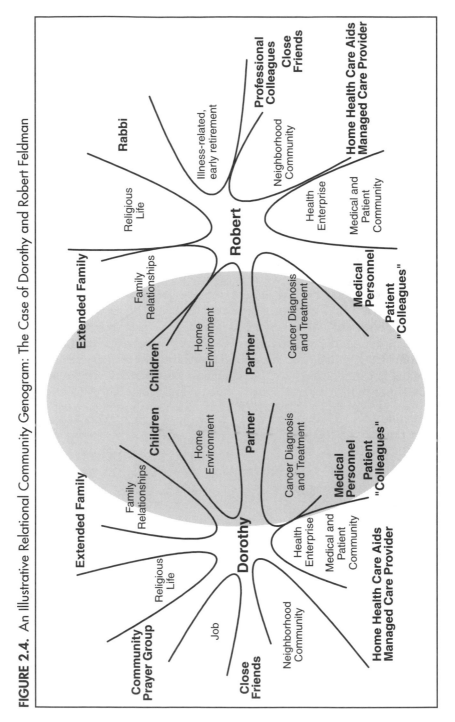

the rabbi and his "patient colleagues" and medical personnel have to Robert are reflected by the open space on the relational diagram.

The therapist then asked Dorothy about the nature of her relationships with her significant others. Again, open spaces reflect active interaction and closed spaces represent closed-off relationships. The client can vary the size of the openings to reflect the perceived quality of the relationship. Notice the differences in openings in Figure 2.4 for Robert and Dorothy.

The diagram was then used to demonstrate what parts of their worlds are less known to the other. For example, notice how Robert's sense of self is far more cut off from significant others and how he relies on only a few others for support, while Dorothy has maintained more open lines of communications with others. For example, they were struck by the different ways they find spiritual support. Robert relies on conversations with the rabbi that focus on preparation for death, while Dorothy finds solace in her prayer group and concentrates on how to enhance living with cancer. Both were impressed with how closed off the family and children are for Robert and how much the family goes through Dorothy to find out what's happening with Robert. It also became clear that they each were experiencing very different feelings while working with the medical facility. Robert focuses on the social and emotional support, while Dorothy deals with the physical caretaking, financial, and insurance aspects of the treatment. These differences were not clear to each other prior to the creation of this community genogram. These findings formed the basis of treatment that focused on how to reconfigure patterns of support for both Robert and Dorothy in order to bring them closer together and achieve a stronger sense of the power of their relationship.

The value of the relational diagram in treatment is that it makes the broader territory in which the couple resides clear for both partners to identify where stress lies and resources can be found within individuals, the family, and the community. If the relationship is strongly connected and each person is familiar with the collective meanings, then these meanings can be shared across their mutual life space. If not, these disconnects in meaning and sense of self and self-in-relation can cause distress. The community genogram provides a concrete method to bring these abstract issues into the here and now of the treatment session. More details on how to construct and analyze relational diagrams will be explored in Chapters 3 and 4.

Others prefer to arrange wooden blocks and represent themselves as geometric shapes, as did Richard and his wife, Anne (see Figure 2.5). Both came from strong fundamentalist backgrounds and had questions about just how much of a role religion would have in their new life. In the first interview, Anne and Richard worked together using 3-D blocks to come to an agreement about how their current situation could be illustrated. Anne was more open to new learnings, while Richard was being persuaded to resume

FIGURE 2.5. An Illustrative Relational Community Genogram Variation: The Case of Richard and Anne Gordan

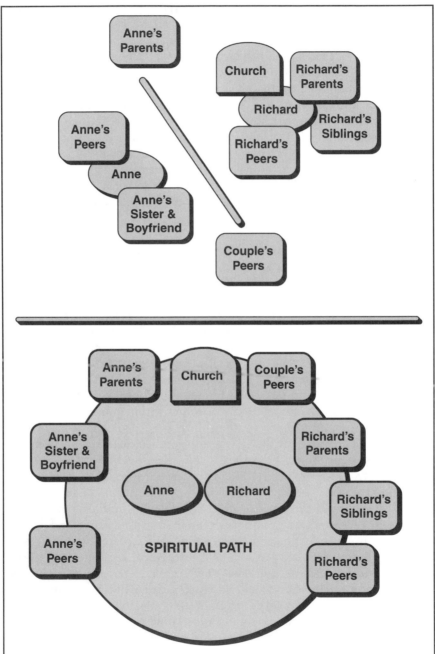

a very active level of participation in the church. Rather than remembering their shared direction, they began to be swayed by sides that spoke of religion but in disparaging terms of the other. So, although they had a strong sense of a common direction when they bonded, as they began negotiating with the world, they were less able to hold their identity and path.

Putting this together with the 3-D blocks, they were able to see that they were walking in different parts of their community and not sharing what they were learning or how they were making sense of things. As the upper diagram in Figure 2.5 demonstrates, the couple was able to see that not sharing their thoughts and separating with others led to an escalation of anxiety and fears about talking to one another. In their words, "we were getting lost."

The couple then used the blocks to come together about the goals for treatment. As can be seen on the bottom of Figure 2.5, Anne and Richard positioned themselves together, in the center of their experience, as the best way to reconnect on their path as a couple and to jointly determine what they could ask for and learn from their community. The couple now could use the church and their family as assets to strengthen their marital relationship rather than to come between them.

These are just some of the flexible ways community genograms can be used to help clients visualize and confront their issues. All are valid and all work, depending on the skill of the counselor to draw out significant themes and events. The Practice Exercise that comes later in this chapter encourages you to use your own creativity to represent a unique visualization of your own community.

THE SIGNIFICANCE OF STRENGTHS AND POSITIVE RESOURCES: THE CASE OF JASON

Jason started treatment talking about how he was affected by the death of his father. The image of his dad and the house he grew up in were still very much with him even though he had moved to a new neighborhood about a year before. Using a community genogram (see Figure 2.6), Jason identified his current life space. The diagram demonstrates how to incorporate graphing tools from other devices such as eco-maps and structural family diagrams. Different types of lines can be used to indicate relationships illustrative of the client's sense of self-in-relation. The heavy dark lines outlining extended families and current inner-city apartment complex means that Jason sees himself cut off from these groups. The dashed lines around current family and current school reflect the fact that Jason is participating in these systems. The dotted lines around his father's legacy and his old neighborhood demonstrate that these elements are very accessible to Jason.

FIGURE 2.6. Using Standard Diagrammatic Assessment Tools to Enhance Community Genograms: The Case of Jason

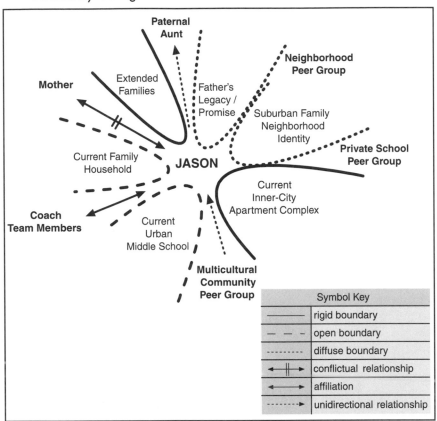

Notice the arrows between Jason and his significant others. The bidirectional arrow indicates that Jason is opening up to his new coach, and the arrow with the crossbars indicates that he experiences tension in his relationship with his mom. The one directional arrow indicates how Jason sees his relationship with his aunt and his new peer group. In the former situation, Jason sees himself reaching out to his aunt but his overtures are not returned. In the latter situation, Jason knows that some classmates have extended a friendly hand but that he has not reciprocated. This diagram helped Jason identify new sources of support and set a direction for the future in his new school.

PRACTICE EXERCISE: IDENTIFYING INDIVIDUAL, FAMILY, COMMUNITY, AND CULTURAL STRENGTHS

The community genogram practice exercise is presented as a way for you to learn more directly how cultural factors, implicit and explicit in the community, underlie individual and family development. We suggest that you first develop your own community genogram and then later use this strategy with others. As you work with the strategy, note that the visual style of the image you develop can be changed to meet your specific needs and experiences. This exercise is, at best, an introduction. To realize the potential of the community genogram, it is essential that you actually engage in the process of the practice exercise.

The exercise has three goals: (1) to generate a personal narrative about you in a community context; (2) to help you generate an understanding of how we all develop in community; and (3) to use visual, auditory, or kinesthetic images as sources of strength. These images of strengths can be called on in life to cope with stressful situations you may encounter in life. In addition, this exercise will help you understand your cultural background as it was transmitted through family and community.

It is not surprising that many individuals, as in the case of Jason, initially focus on their negative experiences as they develop their awareness and stories of how they grew up and now live in a community setting. Although this may be true for you, we ask that you instead focus first on positive strengths and then address the negative aspects that emerge from the analysis of your community genogram.

Step 1: Develop a Visual Representation of the Community

1. Consider a large piece of paper as representing your broad culture and community. It is recommended that you select the community in which you were raised primarily, but any other community, past or present, may be used.
2. Place yourself in that community, either at the center or other appropriate place. Represent yourself by a circle, a star, or other significant symbol.
3. Place your own family on the paper, again represented by the symbol that is most relevant for you. The family can be nuclear, extended, both, or any constellation of individuals that you consider to be "family."
4. Place the important and most influential groups on the community genogram, again representing these by circles or other visual symbols. School, family, neighborhood, and spiritual groups are most often selected. For teens, the peer group is often particularly important. For adults, work groups and other special groups tend to become more central.

5. Connect the groups to you, the focus individual, perhaps drawing heavier lines to indicate the most influential groups.

Step 2: Search for Images and Narratives of Strengths

While you undoubtedly recognize that many individual difficulties and problems arise in a family, community, and cultural context, the community genogram, in its first stages, focuses on positive stories and images. The importance of this point cannot be overstated. The community genogram provides a frame of reference to help the client see self-in-context or family-in-context. The client is asked to generate narratives of key stories from the community where he or she grew up. If relevant, key stories from the present living community may also be important. The emphasis is on positive stories from the community and positive images.

You will find that when this positive approach has been used first, individuals and families have a foundation for exploring more difficult and troublesome areas of their lives. In addition, in a therapeutic setting, you will have a good foundation to help you understand the community, family, and cultural background of the client.

To complete a search for strengths and resources, it is helpful to use the following guidelines:

1. Focus on one single community group or your family. You may want to start with a negative story or image. However, please do no work with the negative until positive strengths are solidly in mind.
2. Develop a visual, auditory, or kinesthetic image that represents an important positive experience. Allow the image to build in your mind and note the positive feelings that occur with the image. If you allow yourself to fully experience that positive image, you may experience tears and/or strong bodily feelings. These anchored body experiences represent positive strengths that can be drawn on to help you deal with difficult current or future issues.
3. Tell the story of the image. You may want to write it down in journal form. You may want to add new images to your community genogram. Elaborate on this image in any way you feel comfortable.
4. Develop at least two more positive images from different groups within the community. It is useful to have one positive family image, one spiritual image, and one cultural image. Again, many will want to focus on negative issues. Hold to the search for positive resources.
5. Summarize the positive images in your own words and reflect on them. What learning, thoughts, and feelings emerge from this analysis? As you think back, what occurs? Your responses outlined in Step 3 below represent deep reservoirs of personal strength for you.

Step 3: Summarize What You Have Learned

To summarize what you have learned about your strengths and resources, answer the following questions:

1. What have I learned about myself?
2. What have I learned about my family?
3. What have I learned about my community?
4. What have I learned about my culture?
5. What have I learned about the concept of self-in-relation?

CONCLUSION: EMPOWERING OUR CLIENTS

Community genograms provide opportunities for clients to become directly involved with the selection and focus of therapeutic goals. It enables them to use their creative and analytic skills to identify sources of strength that can be found in their relationships with the wider community. As such, community genograms may take many forms and paths of analysis, and the issues of boundaries and power arrangements can be mutually explored.

Mental health professionals who are looking for methods to help clients understand their situation from multiple levels and surface new potentialities can use the community genogram as one tool in their therapeutic repertoire. Because of its straightforward process and flexibility, the community genogram can be used with a wide range of clients to draw them into the therapeutic relationship. The drawings, graphics, and insights clients generate are their own and can help initiate or reinforce the journey toward deeper self-understanding and enhanced problem solving.

By exploring the concepts of self-in-relation and family-in-relation with clients, we can create a therapeutic conversation that validates the complexity of their lives yet helps them see significant themes and issues that can be addressed within their current situation. In Chapter 3, we demonstrate the basic components of the prototypic community genogram process and show how these can be used to tap the liberating qualities of community and culture.

Tapping the Liberating Qualities of Culture and Community in Counseling and Therapy

with ANTHONY J. RIGAZIO-DIGILIO

It is not uncommon to hear terms such as *institutional racism*, *systemic prejudice*, or *cultural clash* used to explain the current state of human interaction. On the interpersonal level, cultural norms are often presented as excuses for insensitive and discriminatory behavior in the wider society. Phrases such as "Well, that's the way women are treated in that culture," "Don't blame the racist, blame racism in the society," or "You can't change culture" may lead people to believe that our cultural heritage presents insurmountable obstacles to fight individual and community oppression. Montalvo (1987) referred to the use of this type of reasoning by clinicians as the "stereotypic ethnic vacuum," meaning that by identifying a cultural reason for the existence of a behavior, the behavior is dismissed or minimized. If we only concentrate on the constraining forces of culture and fail to recognize the many potentialities afforded in our cultural heritage, we may be doomed to mindlessly perpetuate these discriminatory practices.

The following major points are emphasized in this chapter:

- **The concept of cultural empathy is explored to create a basis for integrating community factors into treatment.**
- **Boundaries and power are further developed through the use of personal issues related to the self-of-the-therapist.**
- **Cultural Identity Theory is presented as a way to think about the developmental process of adopting a multicultural perspective.**
- **The individual and relational stars, two community genogram prototypes, are detailed and illustrated.**

The community genogram is a tool that can be used to identify the oppressive and discriminatory dimensions of our heritage and to highlight the liberating forces of culture as well. *Culture* has been defined as a mixture of negative and positive behavior patterns, symbols, language patterns, values, institutions, and frames of reference that have been passed on from one generation to the next. Most of us are not fully cognizant of just how many of our actions, values, and ideas are rooted in our cultural traditions.

Only by thoroughly examining our cultural legacy can we maximize the positive aspects and actively work to minimize the negative and unproductive ideas, feelings, and behaviors passed on to us through our families—and communities—of-origin and our life experiences over time and across contexts. By adopting this perspective, our intention is to emphasize the transcendent qualities of culture and community experiences in ways that enable practitioners and clients to make a better world—now and for future generations.

IDENTIFYING CULTURAL INFLUENCES: PRACTICE QUESTIONS

In today's global society, a skill that is at a premium is cultural sensitivity. Business and industry are very interested in attracting employees who possess the ability to understand, appreciate, and work within different cultural settings. In the fields of counseling (D'Andrea, 2000; Pederson, 2000; Sue, Ivey, & Pedersen, 1996; Sue & Sue, 1999) and education (Banks, 2002; Grant & Sleeter, 2002; Nieto, 2001; Smith, 1998) practitioners are expected to demonstrate proficiencies in multicultural competencies. An essential cornerstone of cultural sensitivity is being able to link a person's specific perspectives and ways of viewing the world with their family upbringing and then to connect these perspectives to themes and values held by the person's wider culture. In other words, viewing self and others as cultural beings is essential to effective professional service.

Practice Exercise 3.1

The following series of questions are designed as one way to examine how your family, cultural, and community backgrounds have influenced the values that are part of how you make sense of and participate in the world. Please respond thoughtfully and honestly to each question in order to maximize the learning from this activity.

1. Name your three strongest personal values.
2. Describe two childhood experiences from which you drew one or more of these values to form an opinion about someone that significantly influenced your interactions with or about that person. Include one you remember with fondness and one you remember with regret.

3. Thinking about how values take form, how do you believe these three values were influenced through interactions with your family-of-origin?
4. How did your cultural background influence these values?
5. How did your or your family's position in or exchanges with your communities-of-origin influence these values?
6. List a few life experiences that have significantly supported or challenged these three values and describe the impact these have had on the values as you hold them today.
7. Describe two recent interactions you know were significantly influenced by an opinion or judgment you formed by drawing on one or more of these values to make sense of the exchange. Include one interaction that gives you a sense of pride and one that humbles you.
8. In what ways might you share information about your background and life experiences to help people learn about and appreciate how these three values took form and became a defining part of who you are and how you approach the world?

CULTURAL EMPATHY

Understanding another as a cultural being expands our current definition of empathy. An empathetic attitude is foundational to most counseling and therapy theories (Rogers, 1959) and is central to culturally sensitive helping approaches (Ivey et al., 2002). Often described as "looking at the world through the client's perspective," empathy encompasses the qualities of positive regard, respect, warmth, and genuineness. These qualities have been validated as instrumental components of effective treatment (Anthony & Carkhuff, 1977; Lambert & Bergin, 1994; Sloane & Staples, 1984).

Traditionally, we think of empathy in an individualistic fashion. However, Ivey et al. (2002) have extended the concept to include family and cultural empathy: "Empathy is most often considered an individual issue, but it also rests on an understanding and acceptance of the other person's total life experience. Family and culture deeply intertwine in the clients' lives" (p. 28).

This expanded definition of empathy is predicated on understanding how the individual, family, community, and culture affect client well-being, as well as how clients' positions within these contexts exert influence on definitions of self, self-in-relation, and family-in-context. For example, gender plays a significant role in determining the worldview of a person, as does race, ethnicity, class, and ability. A therapist's empathic response may be different to an African American female than to a Greek American male. The level of perceived and real oppression and privilege each client experiences—in different contexts—needs to be considered in formulating effective treatment plans. The concept of cultural empathy therefore requires those in the helping professions to possess strong awareness of their own cultural values and beliefs, and to use this personal knowledge to understand and appreciate the culture, worldviews, and patterns of oppression and privilege that other groups, families, and individuals experience, overall and in relation to the therapeutic relationship.

Clinicians apply and refine culturally sensitive strategies by listening and watching for the individual, family, community, and cultural references communicated by the client and respond by using words, meanings, and actions that are appropriate within the boundaries of the client's worldview. Community genograms provide opportunities to elicit our clients' worldviews about their multilayered realities and to observe and listen to their personal stories. By using the language and perspectives of the client, a culturally empathic stance is communicated by the counselor. Then, joining together, the client and the counselor can explore the powerful forces that shaped the client's current individual and collective definitions of self-in-relation and family-in-context and identify potential sources of strength and personal power to use to work through the client's presenting issues.

GOING BEYOND CULTURAL EMPATHY: PRACTICE QUESTIONS

Assuming a culturally sensitive disposition is an essential component of establishing a therapeutic alliance. Holding the belief that everyone is a cultural being is necessary, but insufficient to help others realize the potentialities of their heritage. Additionally, clinicians must be prepared to probe the deeper structures and relationships found within the cultural context that have forged the construction of the client's identity and worldview. Knowing a client's most influential relationships and what forms of influence are or were used within these relationships will be important clinical information. The community genogram is one tool that allows clients to graphically illustrate the number and nature of their most influential relationships. In order to examine the nature of these relationships, the two concepts—boundaries and power—introduced in Chapter 2 will be further explored. The following questions are intended to help you examine these two concepts in your life.

Practice Exercise 3.2

1. What group do you belong to that you are most proud of? Please explain.
2. How does your membership in this group affect your sense of your self and self-in-relation?

3. What aspects of your ability to demonstrate cultural empathy were derived from membership in this group?
4. What group did you aspire to join but were never accepted by? In terms of power and boundaries, what did you learn from this experience?
5. In terms of cultural empathy, what did you learn from the experience of not being accepted by this group?
6. What group are you now a member of that you never thought you would be? In terms of power and boundaries, what did you learn from this experience?

EXPLORING BOUNDARIES

Boundaries define relationships. Sometimes we are included inside a boundary, such as being part of the children subgroup of a family, and other times we are outside the boundary, such as not being a member of a particular group. The degree of firmness that defines the relationship can be described as a property of the boundary. Some boundaries are very firm and impenetrable, like the group you wanted to belong to but never could. Other times, boundaries are not very firm and allow considerable cross-flow of interaction, like the boundary between many adult children and their parents.

Boundaries are often defined by the larger culture. Being defined as a child, a sibling, a student, a worker, a spouse, a team member, and a loner are all examples of the types of boundaries placed on us by our culture. Sometimes the boundaries are self-imposed: "I'm an environmentalist" or "I'm a conservative." Other times the boundaries are imposed by others: "You don't belong with us" or "You've passed the admissions criteria, you're in." The nature of the boundaries we draw around ourselves and the boundaries significant others draw around themselves determine our relatedness to one another and deeply influence our sense of self and self-in-relation. How clients perceive their acceptance or rejection within critical relationships in their lives will provide tremendous insight into their current situation and will suggest avenues for overcoming their present difficulties (Rohner, 1986).

An Illustration of Boundaries: Elizabeth

A continuous stressor throughout Elizabeth's life has been a lack of a "true sense of belonging within [her] nuclear family." In Elizabeth's community genogram (see Figure 1.2), this stressor is depicted as a spoke or thread that weaves through the series of interlocking wheels of her life (i.e., adopted family, discrimination, rejecting past, racism, oppression). She states, "I am disappointed greatly by my nuclear family's limitations, but I have learned to accept them as they are, and I have used the experience in a positive fashion in my own life. They have often had great difficulty accepting me, let alone the other relationships [in my life]—this is a pain I must accept and let go of each time it comes up, because otherwise it could cause me to close off to others and then the experience would lead my life in a negative rather than a positive direction."

This lack of acceptance was the result of a combination of factors, situations, and family dynamics. Since not much direct communication with immediate family members is possible—on this issue and other early experiences—she relies on what she has been told by others and by what she remembers. The following is a summary of the dynamic interplay of forces that are associated with the lack of acceptance.

Elizabeth was born the second child and first daughter in a family of three children. She was dark-skinned in a family of white-skinned people, evidence of Native American ancestry. She had a paternal aunt with similar coloring with whom she was closely bonded. Elizabeth explains that, according to what she has been told, her paternal great-great-grandmother was a full-blooded Delaware. Her immediate family for the most part tends to disavow this heritage. The family talks of this great-great-grandmother as "a 'tale' grandpa told." For her family, Elizabeth's skin color was a source of taunting by brother and sister when she was growing up, and something that caused her mother to deny her as a baby. It is a visible indicator of her being different from other members of her family and a very real boundary she had to work through.

EXPLORING POWER

The number of significant relationships and the types of boundaries constructed in each case is only one part of understanding the nature of the client's sense of self-in-relation and family-in-context. A second element has to do with power and influence. All relationships can be considered within a power arrangement. Often, between two parties there is a power differential. Sometimes one party exerts greater influence than another. Power relations can also fluctuate over time and space. For example, parents often exert more power in their relationship with their children, yet there are times and places that the children, even the youngest of them, exercise influence over the parents.

Power and influence can be defined in many ways. Thus far, we have primarily focused on the power of multiple perspectives, cultural heritage, and life experience. Beyond these conceptualizations, however, are issues related to who has the instrumental means to wield the most power and influence through arenas such as status and legitimacy. These issues of social reality are important considerations when determining what layers of intervention can be expected to realistically generate change-inducing perspectives, resources, and options. Legitimized power sources include socioeconomic, educational, and professional status, community standing, political power, and legal resource.

Exploring Personal Power Arrangements: Practice Questions

Clinicians must be prepared to explore the power differentials that exist between clients and significant others or systems, as well as between clients and themselves. Furthermore, clinicians should understand how the real or presumed positions they hold in various relationships with power-differentials influence their perceptions, interactions, and intentions. The next set of questions examines the issue of power arrangements in our lives. The questions should help you consider where you are in your own journey toward realizing the power and resources you may have access to or not, across the various relationships and contexts within which you participate.

Practice Exercise 3.3

1. Who or what group has been most influential in your life? How?
2. For whom or what groups have you exercised significant power and influence? How?
3. Describe a current relationship shaped by a power-differential that constrains you in some significant way. How does this relationship affect your sense of self and self-in-relation?
4. Describe a current relationship in which your power and influence constrains another in some significant way. How does this relationship affect your sense of self and self-in-relation?

The traditional view of power is that A influences B, who is subordinate in the hierarchical structure. We see this on the job when managers influence the way workers conduct their business, in families when parents influence their children's values, and in our communities when more politically connected groups shape governmental policies and practices that affect other community members. This unidirectional view of power and influence is especially true when we consider large aspects of the culture, such as institutional racism, gender bias, and discrimination about sexual orientation.

There are dynamics of power and influence clinicians need to consider when exploring aspects of power and hierarchy at the level of interpersonal exchange between individuals and families. In some relationships most of the power to influence is one-sided in a top-down configuration such as that between a supervisor and employee. In other relationships, the power arrangement is more mutual, going both ways to an almost equal level as is typical in peer relationships. At still other times, the hierarchical relationship only exists because of the power flowing from the bottom up.

Also important to consider are the dynamics of power and influence that occur at the level of exchange between our clients and wider systems. Consider the following questions: "How do social, economic, and political systems operate with respect to particular clients or client groups?" "What has been the historical impact of social forces such as poverty and discrimination on individual and family psychosocial development and life tasks?" "What are the dynamics of power and influence that are contributing to how clients and wider systems define and manage issues that prompt treatment?"

Understanding how power and influence are arranged in our client's significant past and current relationships and communities is important. Obviously, power differentials in the form of social and economic oppression negatively influence the development of personal and collective competencies. So does any dissonance that is created when the demands of the wider community are outside an individual's or family's physical, psychological, cultural, moral, or spiritual sense of self, self-in-relation, or family-in-context, or when wider community, institutional, or sociocultural forces label an individual's or family's familiar ways of perceiving and acting as substandard or deviant. The community genogram can be used to help identify issues of power and influence and to draw out the various situations and relationships in which clients accept power from others, give power to others, or lack the resources to realign power arrangements that impact their functioning and well-being.

Being able to identify the power dynamics operating in these various exchanges is an important step toward determining ways of assuming more power in any situation. Only after the recognition of the actions and expectations of others has been achieved and the available resources for change have been located, can resistance, cooperation, influence, or transformation be enacted. Some clients will not be aware of which people they give their power to. Others may be aware but do not have strategies or resources to change this power relationship. Helping clients and wider networks visualize and make sense of the power relationships that exist within and between individuals, families, communities, institutions, and cultures, as well as the resources available and the points where intervention could initiate relevant power shifts are all important considerations in effective treatment planning.

Finding Personal Power: Elizabeth

Elizabeth described her role within the family with her mother, brother, and sister with whom she was raised as one similar to that of Cinderella: "doing for all of them, but not getting any consideration or return support." She cared, and still cares, for family members during illness and times of need with little reciprocation. While this role was expected of her, and she was and still is considered to be the strong one in her family, little or no sense of belonging "accompanied the 'role.'" It was the role and not her person that was accepted.

The lack of acceptance in her nuclear family and sense of being valued as one who does for others became a part of how Elizabeth saw herself as a child and young adult. Her sense of value was based on what she did or accomplished, rather than being valued as a unique and special person in her own right. She says it took her a long time to learn to accept, love, and believe in herself.

At the age of 28, Elizabeth had an experience that has had a lifelong profound influence on her development. This experience was "a deeply emotional, psychological, and spiritual event" which was accompanied by a moving physical occurrence. Elizabeth uses the term *reborn* to name the experience. The event involved a series of awarenesses that freed Elizabeth from the burdens and constraints of her beliefs about herself, her life, her faith, her family, the functioning of the world, and interactions with others. These awarenesses were accompanied by the physical experience of being "slain in the spirit." Being "slain in the spirit" is difficult to describe, but Elizabeth explains that it is an experience of giving one's physical being to a spiritual power. There is an overpowering sense of being embraced and held by a spiritual force.

As a result of being reborn, Elizabeth's sense of self was enlightened, expanded, strengthened, and made whole. All dimensions of her life were transformed: personal, professional, cognitive, behavioral, and emotional. Using Elizabeth's words, "All together it was a freeing experience, and allowed me to look at life from a much different, more spiritually grounded perspective . . . it gave me a more fluid or expansive worldview, and taught me a great deal about the relativity of things and that there are many different ways to look at or view a subject." Since this experience, Elizabeth reports feeling "secure in my own beliefs, while at the same time feeling totally comfortable with changing my assessment of anything when new information suggests that it makes sense to do so." Her relationship with others changed, allowing her to become closer to the special people in her life.

CULTURAL IDENTITY THEORY: PRACTICE QUESTIONS

As individuals, families, communities, and larger networks grapple with oppressive forces, they travel over this same terrain. Cultural identity theory provides a model for considering the journey clients move through as they work to integrate the multitude of culturally constructed identities of self-in-relation and family-in-context. An overview of cultural identity theory (Cross, 1991; Ivey, 1995; Ivey et al., 2002, Jackson, 1990; Sue & Sue, 1999) is broadly generalized here to consider the developmental pathways individuals and systems use to integrate new aspects of identity (see Figure 3.1). It provides a framework from which therapists can help clients coconstruct meaning about their relationship to others, their family, and their environmental context. Counseling strategies have been developed to enable and liberate the client's positive personal, family, community, and cultural resources (Helms, 1990; Ivey et al., 2002; Jackson, 1975; Ponterotto, Casas, Suzuki, & Alexander, 1995; Sue et al., 1996; White & Parham, 1991).

Examining Your Cultural Identity: Practice Questions

The following questions focus on changes in personal awareness of oppressive forces in the wider culture as these may influence groups positioned apart from the dominant culture.

Practice Exercise 3.4

1. Choose a group that your family belongs to that has experienced some level of cultural oppression or discrimination. At what age did you become aware that society or others harbored negative feelings about this group? In what ways did your family communicate or act as if it wasn't really happening? How did you feel before your realization and after?
2. What was one particularly telling example or situation when you encountered oppression or discrimination in your life? What feelings, images, thoughts, or behaviors did this situation trigger in you?
3. How did you come to label what was going on between you and the oppressing groups? Who was influential in helping identify these dynamics and accept your feelings?

FIGURE 3.1. Cultural Identity Theory

Stage	Actions Needed to Produce Change to Next Stage
1. *Preencounter.* The individual, family, or community group has little focused awareness of themselves as cultural beings within a particular cultural group. Denial and encapsulated experiences with only similar others help reinforce a monocultural perspective of the world.	Help people describe their life experiences and look for examples of oppression and discrimination.
2. *Encounter.* The individual, family, or community group registers the oppression and discrimination. Oppressive and discriminatory experiences penetrate their naivete and initiate a new awareness.	Encourage exploration of self and self-in-relation. Support emotional pride in self and culture.
3. *Immersion.* An identity is solidified with the particular cultural group. Descriptors of how the group may be oppressed or how others may be privileged are often explored in this stage. Often this act of naming is transformative. Awareness shifts to focus on the group itself, its history, its problems, and its goals. The individual, the family, or the community may become encapsulated within their group.	Assist people to name and note the contradictions that emerge between the oppressive behaviors and ideas of others and their own view of the world; learn about the stories of others who have been oppressed in similar and nonsimilar situations; and deal with major emotional change that may occur, often with anger.
4. *Internalization.* A deeper understanding of what it means to be part of a group emerges. Multiple frames of reference can be generated. The individual, family, or community recognizes and accepts the worthwhile dimensions of the predominant culture and fights those aspects that represent oppression. They are able to use all the strengths of the previous three stages.	Encourage exploration and reflection on the contradictions in the system. Continue to emphasize dialogic thought and coinvestigation of reality, and support joint action to transform reality.

4. How did you personally integrate the knowledge that oppression existed outside of yourself and your group? What new definition of yourself did you arrive at from this understanding?
5. How did this one experience with oppression and discrimination move you to action to advocate for others in your group or other groups being oppressed? What new, more powerful frames of reference helped you realize the power of your culture?

Cultural identity theory posits that the movement of consciousness is from a naive lack of awareness to concrete action, to a greater sense of self-in-relation, to society. It is important to understand that all stages possess potentialities and constrictions. The advantages found in Stage 1 are that denial and lack of information may be necessary for the survival and sanity of those individuals, families, communities, and groups that are constantly subject to overt psychological and physical oppression. Conversely, at the fourth level of awareness persons can initiate so many actions, emotions, and ideation about their identity and situation that it can become exhausting and debilitating. Working through these issues is often the focus of counseling and therapy. "Parham points out that 'identity resolution can occur in at least three ways: stagnation (failure to move beyond one's initial identity state), stagewise linear progression (movement from one identity stage to another in a sequential linear fashion), and recycling (movement back through the styles once a cycle has been completed)" (quoted in Ivey et al., 2002, p. 250).

Applying Cultural Identity Theory

Combined with the community genogram, cultural identity theory presents a framework for identifying the personal awareness level of clients in relationship to community and cultural issues. The combination of models provides clinicians with two important diagnostic outcomes. First, based on the level of client cultural awareness, treatment decisions can be tailored to best match and then stretch the clients' current understanding of their situation. Second, it provides information about the stages of development clients will progress through on their journey to find the liberating power of their cultural and community background.

The community genogram is a concrete tool to help clinicians and clients coconstruct images that will move them along the cultural identity spectrum. To examine a client's cultural awareness with the community genogram, a series of questions and tasks may be posed at each stage. For example, when working with the *preencounter stage*, the client may consider these questions: Who and/or what were the dominant forces in your life at this time? What were the protective forces in this environment? What other identities consumed you at that time? How were others operating within your immediate family and community?

Exploring the *encounter stage* can be facilitated by the community genogram data as clients name and note contradictions in experience within a contextual setting. The community genogram can be used to identify key stories and narratives that address the oppressiveness and the liberating aspects of their first awareness that they were part of a cultural group that might be exposed to oppression and/or privilege. During the *immersion stage*, the community genogram can assist clients to relate personal, family, community, or cultural images that can be called upon for strength and affirmative action. During the final stage, the *internalization stage*, the community genogram can be enhanced and modified to include new perspectives, thus helping to sustain the coinvestigation of reality and guide joint action from a dialectic framework.

An Illustration of Cultural Identity Theory: Maya Angelou

Maya Angelou is a woman of many talents: author, poet, editor, dancer, actress, singer, songwriter, teacher, and activist. She is best known for her autobiographical works depicting her life as a black child in the segregated South. The information gathered from her writing, published interviews, and biographies can be used to illustrate how the community genogram and cultural identity theory can be connected.

Preencounter Stage

Cultural identity theory can be used with the community genogram process to describe the life-shaping events for Maya Angelou. In her book, *I Know Why the Caged Bird Sings*, Angelou describes her childhood experiences of being a black girl in the South during the Depression. She describes her parents' divorce; being sent to live with her grandmother in another state; poverty; living in a segregated southern town; threats of violence and rape; a period of not talking; graduating from a training school; working as an adolescent; and having a child at age 16. In her book, Angelou describes her mother and grandmother as strong figures: they worked, were resourceful and independent, and provided nurturance, training, support, and strong role models. The people of her church were an important influence; they nurtured her and gave her a sense of belonging in the community. Literature also was a great influence on Angelou. She writes, "During these years in Stamps, I met and fell in love with William Shakespeare. He was my first white love" (Angelou, 1970, p. 11). These issues are depicted in Figure 3.2 and provide a visual representation of her early life that reflects the preencounter stage of her development.

FIGURE 3.2. Maya Angelou: The Preencounter Stage

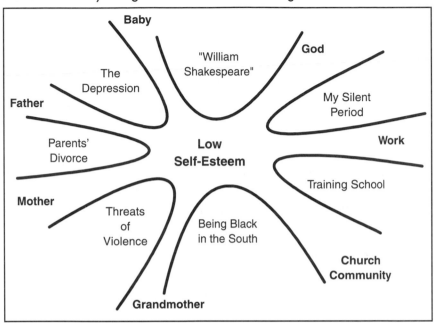

Encounter Stage

Despite the love and nurturance Angelou experienced with her mother, grand-mother, and the church, life was very difficult. The contradictions of Angelou's experience were evident. As a black girl, she was dissatisfied with her physical appearance: kinky hair, small and squinty dark eyes. She remem-bers telling herself, "Wouldn't they be surprised when one day I woke up out of my black ugly dream, and my real hair, which was long and blond, would take the place of the kinky mass that Momma wouldn't let me straighten?" There also was contradiction in her mother's home. A place where she was happy to be with her mother, but unsafe with her mother's boyfriend who raped her at the age of 8. In the southern community, there was the contradiction of living with pride, but being treated with disgust by the poor whites. Maya Angelou describes her childhood this way: "One would say of my life . . . born loser . . . had to be: from a broken family, raped at eight, unwed mother at sixteen. . . . It's a fact but it's not truth. In the black community, however bad it looks, there's a lot of love and so much honor" (Julianelli, 1972). Awareness of these contradictions indicates movement into the encounter stage of cultural identity development.

Immersion Stage

In her 30s, Maya Angelou developed a growing interest in social causes, including civil rights, which is representative of this stage. At the request of Martin Luther King Jr., Angelou served as the northern coordinator of the Southern Christian Leadership Conference. Soon after this involvement, she moved to Africa and there she explored her roots. Angelou wrote, "For Africa to me . . . is more than a glamorous fact. It is a historical truth. No man can know where he is going unless he knows exactly where he has been and exactly how he arrived at his present place." After returning from Africa, Angelou worked to share her knowledge with others by producing a 10-part television series exploring African traditions in American life. Her writing projects have been vehicles to express her desire for change in terms of civil rights (Goodman, 1972).

Internalization Stage

Maya Angelou continues to grow and expand her perspectives through writing. Spirituality has been an important influence in Maya Angelou's life. Her spirituality has provided her a nurturing community in which to develop and gain rhythm that she uses in her writing. Her views on religion show an integration of a number of perspectives (see Figure 3.3). In response to a question about how religion has affected her, Angelou said:

> I have a great attachment—that's such a weak word—a gratitude for the presence of God. I grew up in a Baptist church so I prefer and understand Baptist ritual, but all roads lead to Rome. If you know that, you don't put value judgments on [religions]. You use the wisdom of all of them. We are a community of children of God, whether we admit it or not, whether we call it God or the Creator or the Source or Nature. We're a community. (Toppman, 1983, p. 143)

It is this community that Angelou is interested in and struggles to understand and to be an active and contributing member of—all evident of the internalization process.

THE COMMUNITY GENOGRAM: A CLINICAL TOOL FOR CULTURAL LIBERATION

The community genogram can be used to elicit self-in-relation information at all stages of the cultural identity model. Images and sensations, stories, reflections, and narratives can be used to help clients coconstruct empowering representations through the exploration of the community genogram data.

FIGURE 3.3. Maya Angelou: The Internalization Stage

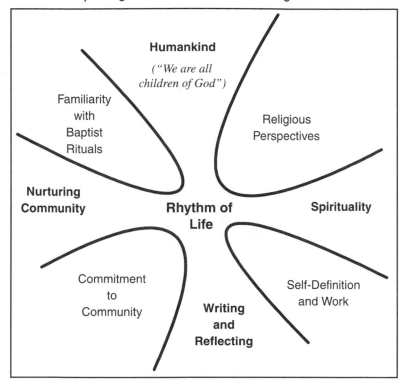

In this fashion, the community genogram is a therapeutic procedure that can be used to liberate the potential of our client's cultural heritage. To illustrate this, we introduce a prototypical community genogram graphic. Developed by Lois Grady, this community genogram takes the form of a star that can be used to illustrate individual or relational narratives.

The Basic Components of the Individual and Relational Star Diagrams

Figure 3.4 represents the central components of the *star diagram* which serves as a suggested template for eliciting the individual, family, relational, and wider contextual information basic to a community genogram. This diagram can be seen as a graphic illustration of a time-slice within a client's life, in the context of the predominant culture and society inhabited at that time.

FIGURE 3.4. The Basic Components of Individual and Relational Star Diagrams: Embayments, Channels, and Context of Collective Exchange

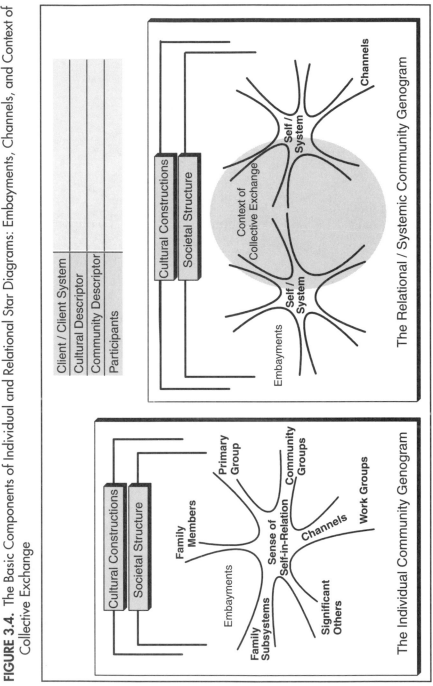

| Client / Client System |
| Cultural Descriptor |
| Community Descriptor |
| Participants |

The Relational / Systemic Community Genogram

The Individual Community Genogram

Any number of time-slice individual or relational star diagrams can be constructed, depending on what phases of life, stages of cultural identity, or primary contexts seem most relevant to understanding and responding to the presenting issue and to facilitating continued growth and adaptation. In Chapter 4 we will demonstrate how to use the star diagram over the life span.

The central components of the star diagram include the client, influential family members and subsystems, significant others and groups, major cultural and community events, and personal and family experiences. In other words, this community genogram reflects the focus of treatment, including the major contributors and construers of the problem. The aim is to focus on those components which have influenced the client's internalization of the self-in-relation identity at a particular stage of development and in a particular predominant context.

Let us first look at the individual community genogram. At the *center* of the star is the client uniquely positioned within and uniquely interacting with societal structures and cultural constructions. The *embayments* of the star are comprised of the major environmental influences (e.g., cultural and community events, personal and family experiences, legacies, and patterns) that impinge upon and influence the client's perception of self and self-in-relation. The number of embayments are arbitrary and the depth and size are indicative of the power of their influence. The *points* of the star encompass influential family members and subsystems, as well as significant others and primary groups who serve to connect the client to wider contexts. Again, there can be any number of individuals, subsystems, and groups identified as significant by the client.

Now notice how the points of the star are elongated and opened to embrace the significant individuals, subsystems, or groups who serve to connect the client, to differing degrees, with experiences and relationships in the larger world. These elongations form channels between the embayments. Channels can be broad, narrow, or closed off to illustrate the relationship with that significant other. Together, the embayments and channels of the star can be used to illustrate issues of boundaries and power within the client's depictions.

The star diagram illustrates how the interactions of a client with major environmental influences and with significant persons, subsystems, and groups affect growth by promoting or preventing opportunities for change. This community genogram can then represent the degree of involvement the client has with community events, sociopolitical and economic realities, and interpersonal relationships. Thus, the star diagram as a metaphor is both a static image and an image that illustrates potential consequences of growth and change. During the course of therapy, the clinician and the client can use the diagram to dialogue about how different desired changes in relationships or in environments will effect one another.

Let us turn our attention to the relational/systemic community genogram depicted in the second box of Figure 3.4. It shows how common contextual and interpersonal situations can affect more than one person or system. It illustrates how significant individuals, subsystems, or groups around the rim of the star have a similar star form. Sometimes these significant others share similar environmental influences, experiences, and people, which are identified by the shaded area called the "context of collective exchange." They also will have a varied array of uncommon environments, experiences, and significant relationships. Embayments are used to illustrate how the wider contextual realities and events also influence the clients' life space. The point of knowing this is to recognize that clients have multilayered realities that clinicians should strive to understand and bring into the process of treatment. In this way, clinicians and clients can look at ways to expand and enrich a client's star by bringing other persons and environments into the therapeutic process that might not otherwise be considered.

The coding box is added to the diagram to illustrate the importance of systematic notation. Keeping track of how star diagrams are used to explore specific situations of cultural and community import is essential to best practice. Noting whose perception is captured and who were the participants will also facilitate later discussions of each community genogram throughout the counseling process. Having different members of the client system depict similar situations is a concrete method of raising differences of perceptions. Keeping track of whose perceptions are reflected with information about the specific time-slice is essential to the coordinated use of these diagrams to punctuate progress, highlight similarities and differences in perceptions, and set therapeutic goals.

A Star Diagram for an Individual: Evelyn

The community genogram helps us focus on both the client's sense of self and self-in-relation. Consider Evelyn, a 6th-grade student of Mexican descent who lives in a single-parent household in a college town in the Northeast. Her family is very active in the Pentecostal church. Regardless of the issues that Evelyn or any client presents, understanding the cultural background and social support network can be helpful in conceptualizing counseling and treatment planning. In the following dialogue, the therapist is helping Evelyn use the star diagram (see Figure 3.5) to search for areas of strength and support that she can call upon when peers at school are teasing her. Evelyn's issues are typical of the early encounter stage of cultural identity development.

FIGURE 3.5. An Illustrative Community Genogram: The Case of Evelyn

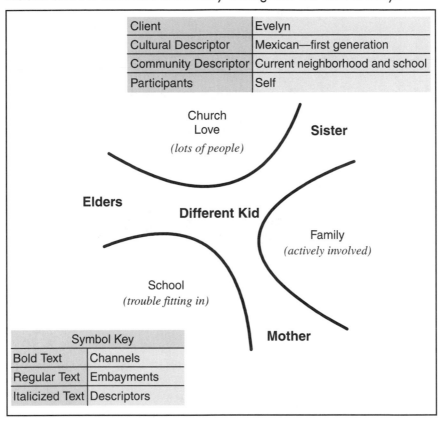

Client	Evelyn
Cultural Descriptor	Mexican—first generation
Community Descriptor	Current neighborhood and school
Participants	Self

Symbol Key	
Bold Text	Channels
Regular Text	Embayments
Italicized Text	Descriptors

Therapist: Last time we looked at how your family can support you, today let's take a look at the church and maybe close your eyes and think of it . . . get an image in your mind. The church. How would you describe it?

Evelyn: Very homey.

Therapist: Homey.

Evelyn: A lot of people, you know, that I know, they're always there for me.

Therapist: Okay, so when you think about your church, you see a lot of people that you know, it's homey, it feels comfortable.

Evelyn: Mmm-hmm.

Therapist: And they're there for you, if you need them. That feels good.

Do you remember one specific thing that comes to mind at all when you think about the church?

Evelyn: Well, yeah! There's one time [small laugh] when I was having an argument with my sister, so, you know, the elders there, they're always there for me and so I can just go to them and they always cheer me up and they always figure things out for me, and . . .

Therapist: Oh, so . . . so that when you have an argument with your sister that you can go and talk to somebody else, even outside your family. But it's really sort of part of your family . . .

Evelyn: Yeah.

Therapist: . . . it sounds like, at your church, you can go to the elders and talk with them. And get some ideas on how to work with your sister a little bit better.

Evelyn: Yeah, every time I think of the church, I think of it crowded and all these people and, like, everywhere I go, people are saying, "Hi, Evelyn," I know everyone. It's just a nice feeling.

Therapist: Oh! Nice feeling. And where do you feel that feeling, from the church? Where do you feel that in your body?

Evelyn: Everywhere! I just feel happy!

Therapist: Everywhere. It makes you feel happy.

Evelyn: Yeah.

Therapist: So that's another strength and resource you can bring with you. All the time. You can think, "Well, my church is with me. All the people in my church are with me. So if I have problems in school or somebody comes up and starts teasing me or I'm not getting along too well, I have my church family with me, and you can think about all those wonderful people." And all through your body you feel the church, and all the people in the church, supporting you and surrounding you with love.

Evelyn: [small laugh] Yeah, that's right.

Therapist: How did that feel for you, to talk about that?

Evelyn: That felt good.

Therapist: We focused primarily on your church. That they're with you.

Evelyn: Helps me to appreciate the things that I have. And that, you know how good it is. I have my church with me. Even if the kids at school tease me, I have these people to support me.

A Relational Star Diagram for a Family: The Morris Family

A Jamaican family living in the Bronx, New York, the Morrises were being investigated by protective services for alleged neglect and abuse. School personnel filed a suspected child abuse report when Rose came to school with a bruised upper arm. The report included information that Leon's attendance also had dropped precipitously in this year. The first three months of involvement with the protective service worker were contentious, and the Morris family obtained a legal advocate to stop "further intrusion" by the Protective Service Agency. To mediate this case, a counselor was called in to consult with the parents and the protective service worker.

In the first interviews, the consultant introduced the community genogram as a way to capture the contextual dimensions that could expand the definition of the problem and identify more options and resources for its resolution (see Figure 3.6). The left hand star of the community genogram depicts the social, political, and institutional influences (embayments) and significant professionals and clients (channels) that the protective service worker believed contributed to her case formulation and management. The important cultural, community, institutional, and family influences defined by the parents were placed as embayments on the right-hand star, and significant others related to these influences were situated in the corresponding channels. The stars were then situated in relation to one another. The embayments and channels identified as part of the context of collective exchange, designated by the shaded area, were placed in the middle of the graphic to demonstrate the forces and resources influencing both the family and the worker. Influences unique to each were situated on the outside of this common point of reference.

Using the diagram, the cultural and family-of-origin patterns influencing the parent-child relations in the Morris family were reviewed, as were the criteria used by the worker to evaluate parent-child relationships. It was clear that the Morris family's behavior was consistent with family functioning in Jamaica. In Jamaica, it's not unusual for males to turn to the world outside school early in their teens and for girls to be more academically oriented. Leon was working with his father in a local gas station and was missing school. "In Jamaica, this happens all the time. It's how we survive. I was working on the farm since I was 8," Trevor noted. Furthermore, physical discipline is common in Jamaican families. Parents demonstrate their love for their children by "keeping a firm hand on things."

It was also clear that the information and standards used by the protective service worker to evaluate the parenting conditions in the Morris family did not address cultural dimensions of parenting or take into account the educational and economic conditions in the Jamaican community. As Trevor and Maxine's parenting and the worker's evaluation were discussed in context, the differences between the cultural parenting patterns of Jamaican and American families became clear. This helped facilitate

FIGURE 3.6. An Illustrative Systemic Community Genogram: The Case of the Morris Family

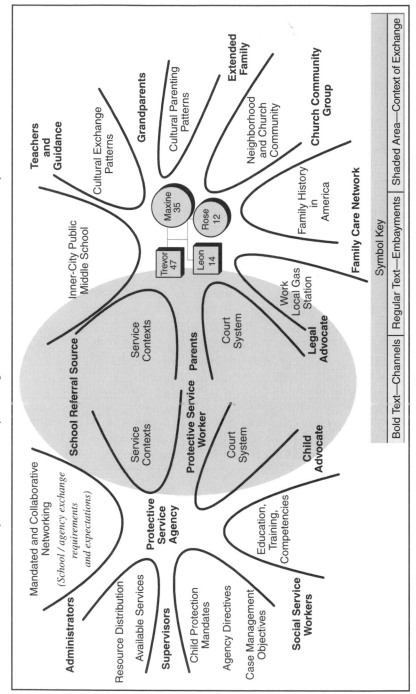

a discussion about ways to address differences that are not governed by the concept of deviance. The right side of the diagram introduced a range of resources and affiliations beyond the specifics of the referral that served to identify the Morris family. The economic situation Jamaican families live within the wider community was also discussed. It was pointed out that not many Jamaican male students graduate from school and that those who do complete school seldom secure meaningful employment. For example, after three years in the United States, Trevor was still working for low wages at a local gas station. School and protective service personnel had not considered these other resources or the financial hardships as foreground factors in their assessment of or work with the Morris family up to this point. The need to create community supports for the Morris family and, in fact, others who had gone through similar exchanges became more evident as the exploration continued.

The diagram also helped inform the parents about the institutions and officials who were involved with their case. The parents were able to see the protective service worker in a new light and realized that certain behaviors were less accepted in the United States. They had other family members who migrated before them and experienced similar entanglements and they did not want to repeat these problems. They could see that in the United States things would have to be different.

The Morrises' ability to understand their cultural situation and to work toward changes in both their family patterns and the wider social context is indicative of the internalization stage of cultural identity. Rather than continuing the legal actions, the Morrises were able to understand how to work with the protective service worker to have their case terminated, acquired a deeper appreciation for their cultural heritage, and learned to adapt to cultural norms about parent-child interactions expected in the United States. The protective service agency supported a grant aimed at developing education and vocational training for the Jamaican community. With the help of their church, Trevor and Maxine began to organize a support group for families experiencing the same economic conditions. School officials contacted a local community college to establish an after-school tutoring program. Leon returned to school, and new disciplinary methods were designed to communicate the family's values of respect, hard work, strong effort, and politeness to the children.

Practice Exercise: Constructing Your Own Star Diagram

To assist in moving from theory to practice, we now ask you to create another community genogram, this time using a star diagram to explore another time-slice of your life.

Phase 1

Select a very influential period of your development and visually represent the primary community you resided in during that time.

1. Use a large piece of paper to represent your broad culture and community at the time period you selected. For this exercise, select a community in which you lived during a time when your cultural identity truly broadened. Place descriptors at the top of the page that describe your cultural context, and place community descriptors directly below.
2. Draw a large circle that represents your specific life space within the larger community. This circle does not have to be in the center of the page. You may place it anywhere on the page, depending on how you perceive your relationship with, or position within, the larger community.
3. Place yourself at the center of your circle designating the middle of the star shape that you will create.
4. Working along the outer edge of the circle, write the names of those significant persons who were influential during your development at this time. These persons may be named separately (e.g., mother, minister, best friend, significant relative, neighbor) or collectively (e.g., parents, siblings, friends, teachers, community groups). Place them around the circle to represent their own relationship with one another.
5. Place the most important and significant influences and experiences in the embayments protruding from the outer circumference into the middle of the circle. Use the size and length of the embayment to represent the degree of significance these influences had. As you draw these embayments, consider the channels that are being formed. Do these represent the appropriate openness between you and the significant persons you have listed on the outside of the circle?

Phase 2

Search for images and narratives of strengths. Again, in the first stages of this search, your analysis should focus on positive stories and images.

1. Focus on one single positive community experience or a positive relationship with a significant person that helped you become more aware of your cultural identity.
2. Develop a visual, auditory, or kinesthetic image that represents that important experience or relationship. Allow the image to build in your mind and note the positive feelings that occur.

3. Tell the story of your image. You may want to write it down in journal form or share it with a friend or other family members.
4. Develop at least two more positive images from different groups within your community genogram that were influential in your cultural development.

Phase 3

Integrate the personal meaning of your images.

1. Summarize the positive images you have generated in your own words and reflect on these. Summarize your learning, thoughts, and feelings. As you think back, what occurs? What themes do you notice across experiences?
2. Compare how the positive images are still evident in your current life. How do the strengths derived from these experiences help you gain multiple perspectives about your self-in-relation?
3. Reflect on how you use these strengths in interpersonal, professional, and other significant contexts. To whom in your current life space are you passing on this cultural power?
4. How can the information gleaned from the web diagram of your community genogram be used to improve your counseling skills?
5. How can the community genogram be used in counseling to assess, join, and enable your clients?

CONCLUSION: LIBERATE THE POTENTIAL OF INHERITED CULTURAL LEGACIES

As we develop, our boundaries extend to include wider contexts of exchange, and we rely, in part, on our cultural legacies to make sense of and participate in these various contexts. Moreover, the exchanges are shaped by dimensions of relatedness and power that may elicit or constrain our resources and capabilities. The community genogram can be used to understand and account for these factors in counseling and therapy.

Cultural identity development theory offers a framework for counselors and clients to examine issues of heritage and context. Talking with clients about the different stages can uncover debilitating and maximize liberating potentials inherent in their relationship with their cultural legacy. This analysis can then be applied to their current situation to help inform culture-sensitive plans for treatment.

The community genogram frames those issues prompting treatment as existing within the relationships within and among individuals, families, and the wider environment. This frame can be used to explore the subtle and overt forces that come to influence individual and family development, cultural identity development, life tasks, and that elicit or constrain current resources capabilities, and functioning. This broader territory can be used to explore the various factors contributing to the issues presented in treatment and help determine the levels of intervention that will potentially access instrumental and relational resources and generate a sense of shared responsibility, mutual understanding, and problem solving.

CHAPTER 4

Exploring Life Span Development with the Community Genogram

Exploration of the community genogram is a very emotional, dramatic, yet practical clinical strategy. Beyond the powerful insights it can generate in counseling, it helps you understand the special cultural background of the client. It provides information about how clients conceive of and communicate their sense of self-in-relation or family-in-relation. Additionally, it serves as a reservoir of positive experiences which can be drawn on to help you and your clients throughout therapy. In subsequent chapters we will demonstrate how community genograms can be used in individual and family counseling. But first, let's explore how a community genogram can be used as a therapeutic strategy to represent clients' development over their life span. In this chapter we will emphasize the following points:

- **How to use community genograms to track personal and familial growth over time**
- **How to construct a culturally sensitive model of practice using community as a key dimension**
- **How the Multicultural Cube can assist in the interactive assessment of client issues and the identification of counselor bias**
- **How to construct community genograms that reflect life span issues**

VALUES AND TRAITS: PRACTICE QUESTIONS

Each individual has a unique genetic endowment and disposition. Each family has a unique composition, structure, and interactional style. Concurrently, each individual and family has different positions of power in various social and temporal contexts. The way these different individual, family, and wider contextual variables interact over time can account for how clients individually and collectively experience, interpret, and react to their life tasks and events. Multiple community genograms can be used to capture this developmental process. The following questions demonstrate how to focus on particular personal qualities over time.

FIGURE 4.1. A Community Genogram for Elizabeth: A Composite of Major Themes

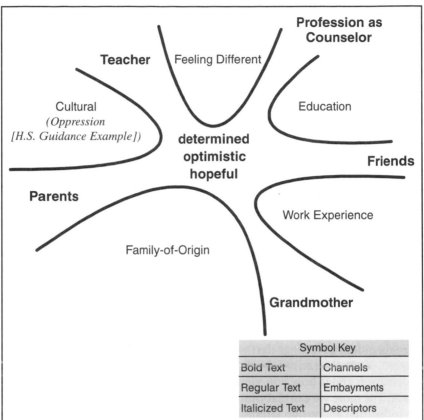

before I accepted it fully as something that just was, and began to understand that as a child I didn't feel I belonged anyplace."

Elizabeth lists her grandmother, her education, her friends, and experiences that validated her self-worth. These various influences encouraged Elizabeth as a young person to "peel away [her] defenses and examine her values." She had a sense of awareness about what was going on in her family. "My critical thinking skills better enabled me to see and understand the denial games that were going on." Elizabeth's intellectual skills and insight have allowed her to come to a sense of resolution about her family issues. These abilities also have served her well in her profession as a counselor, educator, and trainer.

Optimism and unrelenting hopefulness are strengths apparent through all of Elizabeth's discussions about life. "There's always the potential for positive change and growth. This is evident in my own transformation. It's never too late to help someone or for someone to turn their life around."

Elizabeth has a strong sense of determination and personal responsibility. This is illustrated in her continual movements forward and desire to be an instrument of change even in the face of adversity. For example, Elizabeth found that in high school the guidance counseling available was ineffective. Elizabeth thought that it needed to be improved and decided "to be a part of trying to change it." She became a teacher and then went on to get a degree in guidance. She did this despite the fact that little or no support was provided by her family. More recently, Elizabeth has focused her attention as a counselor on issues of oppression and discrimination in the U.S. culture.

Elizabeth has not only used her strengths to promote her own development, but has also devoted her life to helping others. Elizabeth has been able to use her difficult experiences in her nuclear family to develop skills and strengths to assist others with similar experiences. She states, "Since 'I've been there, done that too' for so much of what disturbs folks, and I've worked it out for myself, I can 'walk' with them into their pain and not worry as much about opening up wounds within myself I was not aware of."

USING THE MULTICULTURAL CUBE

Using interactive graphic assessment strategies, such as the community genogram, with diverse clientele requires a counseling approach that values and examines the unique interpretations our clients bring to treatment. Helping clients select and carefully explore their issues, in their own natural language, is a central thrust of most therapies. To assist clinicians and clients to select foci for coinvestigation, Ivey and his colleagues (Ivey, D'Andrea, Ivey, & Simek-Morgan, 2002; Ivey, Gluckstern, & Ivey, 1992) developed the multicultural counseling cube.

Culturally Sensitive Counseling

The Multicultural Cube (Ivey, 1991, 1995, 2000; Ivey et al., 2002) is grounded in the theory of multicultural counseling (Sue et al., 1996) and developmental counseling and therapy (Ivey, 2000; Rigazio-DiGilio, 1994) and helps organize possible areas for the initiation and continuation of culturally responsive treatment. The cube contains three major domains that need to be considered in assessing client need and designing tailored treatment plans:

(1) the locus of treatment, (2) multicultural issues, and (3) level of cultural identity development, all as presented by the client.

The cube juxtaposes these three domains that, when interrelated, provide a holistic composite of potential therapeutic issues (see Figure 4.2). All clients present combinations of multicultural issues, and different issues may predominate therapeutic conversations at different times. Helping clients view their issues embedded within a contextual backdrop helps them see the multiple communities within which they and their families live. "*Multicultural* is a way to talk of the many cultures within each of us. We are not solely ethnic/racial beings" (Ivey et al., 2002, p. 245). We also are individuals with our own sense of self, and simultaneously, we are social beings with our sense of self-in-relation. We belong to many cultures that extend within and across the domains at the top of the cube which coalesces as an "individual's unique personal history—a distinctive personal culture" (p. 245).

In the Multicultural Cube, "you see that everyone participates in multiple cultural and social groups" (Ivey et al., 2002, p. 245). Notice the placement of the family in relation to the individual; this reflects the family's role as the mediating context between individual family members and the outer world.

For many clients their relationship with a particular culture may not be fully integrated. The level of cultural identity development across the right side of the cube is used to help guide the integration process. "At one point, ethnic/racial issues may be important, but at another point, one's physical ability or economic class may be the central issue related to the counseling and therapy process. We are all multicultural beings and all of us are deeply affected by our multicultural status" (Ivey et al., 2002, p. 245).

Counselors can use the cube to help clients understand the numerous, and specifically the most influential, individual and social influences affecting their current situation. And when making these connections across the cube, help clients be ever vigilant for untapped or underutilized resources. The value of the cube is to help situate the issues of the client within a particular territory of the cube. Some of our client issues will reside deep with the intersection of only two variables, such as the family dealing with the terminal disease for a 42-year-old mother of 5-year-old twins.

There are other times when the area under consideration assumes a much wider spread across the domains. Consider the territory affected when working with an Arabic American family whose son is in prison and not permitted to have contact with the outside. This client's issues reach far beyond the normal developmental stress of launching a son into the world. In this way, the cube can be used to first identify, and then work within and across the most efficacious cells of the cube to explore options and resources that have been underutilized or not previously considered.

FIGURE 4.2. The Multicultural Cube

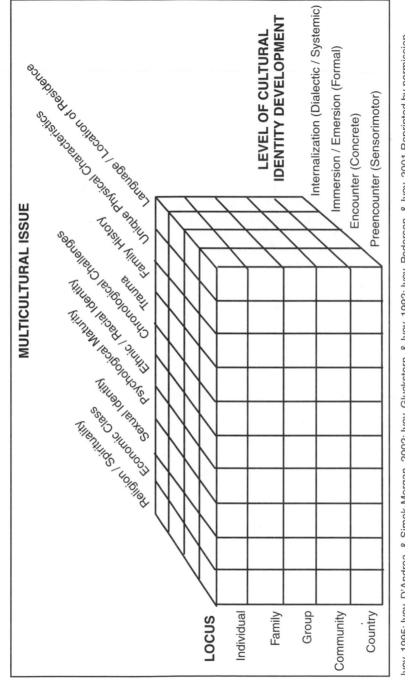

MULTICULTURAL ISSUE

Religion / Spirituality
Economic Class
Sexual Identity
Psychological Maturity
Ethnic / Racial Identity
Chronological Challenges
Trauma
Family History
Unique Physical Characteristics
Language / Location of Residence

LOCUS

Individual
Family
Group
Community
Country

LEVEL OF CULTURAL
IDENTITY DEVELOPMENT

Internalization (Dialectic / Systemic)
Immersion / Emersion (Formal)
Encounter (Concrete)
Preencounter (Sensorimotor)

Ivey, 1995; Ivey, D'Andrea, & Simek-Morgan, 2002; Ivey, Gluckstern, & Ivey, 1992; Ivey, Pedersen, & Ivey, 2001. Reprinted by permission.

Domain 1: Locus

Along the left side of the cube, the locus of treatment is differentiated. Locus of treatment is not the same as the people who compose the client system. For example, you could be working with an individual, but the locus could be changes the client would like to see happen at the family or group level. Conversely, you may be working with a family who has focused on the needs of one individual. Knowledge of the client's locus helps determine the type of treatment modalities and plans of intervention that will best address the issues promoting treatment.

Traditional theories and even postmodern narrative models of counseling and therapy often locate the delivery of treatment at the individual and family level, even if it is at odds with the client's own locus. Therapists must have access to a wider array of services in order to better tailor culturally sensitive treatment to the specific needs of their clients. Underutilized interventions, beyond the number of clients that comfortably fit within the counseling office, may need to be initiated to effectively resolve concerns that focus on larger social groups. While this may sound overwhelming, remember that it was as recent as the cybernetic revolution of the 1950s and 1960s that the mental health field began to seriously attend to family dynamics. The community genogram can be a tool to widen our therapeutic lens and to incorporate ecosystemic theories, such as those espoused by Adler (1926), Attneave (1982), Auerswald (1983), Bowen (1978), Bronfenbrenner (1979), Jung (1935), Kelly (1955), Minuchin (1974), and White (1989)—all of whom have stressed the importance of intervening at the group, community, and societal levels.

Domain 2: Multicultural Issues

Across the top of the cube are the types of multicultural issues clients may bring up in counseling. Again, traditional therapeutic models tend to take a narrow perspective and overemphasize symptom relief at physical, affective, and socioeconomic levels. Issues relating to domains such as spirituality, ethnicity, gender, physical trauma, and language are often referred to specialists and are not viewed as important by third-party payers and insurance groups. Consequently these issues receive little attention in general models of helping. Community genograms can, however, highlight these underrecognized issues and raise them to a conscious level for assessment and treatment planning purposes.

Domain 3: Level of Cultural Identity Development

Clients also vary as to their awareness of how these multicultural issues affect their lives as discussed in Chapter 3. The level of cultural identity development (see Figure 3.1), listed along the right side of the cube, integrates the four phases of client awareness into our diagnostic and formulation process. Ranges of awareness differ for each client by multicultural issue and locus. For example, a female client may be at the internalization level on issues about aging in her extended family because of the recent deaths of many elder family members, but may simultaneously be at the preencounter stage about gender issues happening in her new job environment. A family might be able to identify and name the school's reaction to their daughter's cerebral palsy, but may become confused when they encounter the school's strong recommendation to medicate their son due to symptoms school officials suggest are representative of an attention deficit disorder.

Developmental Criteria for Moving Within the Cube

Making clinical decisions about where and how to access potential resources designated in the Multicultural Cube can be overwhelming without guiding principles. Therapeutic assumptions undergirding developmental counseling theory (DCT) (Ivey, 1991, 1995, 2000; Rigazio-DiGilio, 1994) can assist clinicians to design culturally sensitive, client-centered treatment plans.

First, consider the cube as a large map that presents an expanded vision of the therapeutic terrain. Not all areas of the map need to be explored or considered during the course of treatment, but a few areas most probably will be examined significantly. DCT advocates that clinicians "lead by following," using the concerns and themes clients present as the path of treatment. Matching treatment decisions to client language and worldview is an integral component of DCT.

However, leading by following can be confusing if clinicians do not have a larger scheme to make sense of client narratives. The cube provides this scheme. It is possible to ascertain where client concerns are most highly focused within the cube, and to help explore the potential for change within those areas. If, and when, the therapeutic resources begin to dwindle, or begin to prove ineffective, other areas can be examined in a systemic fashion. Rather than randomly skipping around the cube trying to find the essential therapeutic material, clients and clinicians can coconstruct narratives that might draw on new areas of the cube that would prove to be more successful. For example, if an individualistic locus about a past trauma is not helpful in facilitating movement along the multicultural awareness continuum, the clinician and client might find that a broader locus might be more helpful, or choose another time period over the life span to examine the same issue.

There are four DCT assumptions that offer criteria that can be used to make decisions about how clinicians and clients might explore the many aspects of the cube.

1. Assume a Developmental, Nonpathological Perspective

Clinicians should use the cube initially to chart the strengths of clients and involved systems. In doing so, clinicians can help clients realize how to activate and reorganize these strengths in light of current issues. Instead of focusing solely on the problem, its causes, and its consequences, DCT emphasizes a positive stance that assumes all clients and involved systems possess resources that can be accessed to resolve current difficulties and to prepare clients for future developmental and situational transitions. Coconstructing multiple, time-specific community genograms helps to depathologize client issues and to realize times in which the same issues were sources of strength and renewal.

2. Tailor the Treatment to the Idiosyncratic Worldview of the Client

Clinicians should begin treatment by listening to the specific language that clients use to present their issues. Remember the type of language you used to express yourself in answering questions at the beginning of this chapter. Just as you use a predominant narrative form, either images, stories, abstract concepts, or analyses, our clients also have a predominant way of looking at their world. For some clients, their language will communicate a more concrete or feeling orientation to the world, while for others, their language may represent a more abstract or suppositional orientation. DCT uses the terms *sensorimotor*, *concrete*, *formal*, and *dialectic/system* orientations to help classify client's worldview. These terms are inserted in Figure 4.2 to signify the relationship between cultural identity theory and DCT. Treatment initially needs to be crafted within clients' worldview using narrative styles that are compatible with their own. Only after genuine joining and strong understandings of this worldview have been communicated can clinicians initiate movement, through modification of the narrative style, to enhance, expand, and challenge the parameters inherent in clients' worldview.

3. Broader Access to Resources Within the Cube Is Better

Research (Rigazio-DiGilio & Ivey, 1995) on DCT has demonstrated that the potential for therapeutic growth is enhanced when clients can tap a wide array of personal and interpersonal resources, view issues from a variety of perspectives, and see multiple options for change. Oftentimes clients will present a very narrow and rigid perspective regarding the issues prompting treatment. Helping them realize that underrecognized or never-utilized resources exist within themselves and their environments is an essential goal of DCT. Community genograms can be used as maps to discuss potential areas for new and underutilized resources to be accessed.

4. Recognize and Appropriately Respond to the Power Arrangements Clients Present

A client's status within the sociopolitical and economic environment directly affects access to potential resources. The relationship between the client and the predominant culture must be considered in the coconstruction of treatment plans. We live in an oppressive culture that affects all members of society—even those who initially appear privileged. The relationship of clients to their wider culture establishes a power differential that will affect the type of resources available within the environment. The multicultural cube can help identify issues of power in a wide spectrum of contexts that can be examined in the community genograms coconstructed in treatment. This information can be factored into culturally sensitive, client-centered treatment plans and can be used to determine multiple intervention points (e.g., individual, family, institution, community).

Together, the multicultural cube and the constructs from DCT offer a comprehensive method to use community genograms in treatment. By exploring with clients how their issues develop over time in relation to others and how their worldview of their situation can be enhanced to include unrecognized strengths and resources, clinicians can enable clients to assume multiple perspectives on treatment issues and identify multiple options for change. Oftentimes, clients' historical and interconnected elements are best illustrated through a series of community genograms depicting stages of development over their life span.

A LIFE SPAN COMMUNITY GENOGRAM

A life span community genogram illustrates how individuals, families, and wider contexts change over time. Should it be therapeutically prudent to construct life span community genograms, a graphic that illustrates lineage connectors can be used to assist clients to conceptualize their developmental journey (see Figures 4.3–4.7). Thus a series of star diagrams—one for each life phase—can be metaphorically stacked and fit into a sphere with the central column representing the changing self and self-in-relation. These star diagrams can also be used with couples and families—as will be discussed in detail in Chapter 6—but here we will focus their use with individuals.

Individual Star Diagrams

There are five basic star diagrams that represent five different time-slices. For individuals, the basic components of each web differ by the age of the client. These would include the *young child*, the *older child*, the *young adult*, the *adult*, and the *senior adult*. Although these age-referenced stages are used to illustrate the basic prototypes for the community genogram, clinicians and clients can determine the most significant life phases to depict in each star.

Young Child

Infants and preschool children have a relatively limited number of channels connecting to significant others in their lives, such as parents and caretakers (see Figure 4.3). The embayments might be limited to the environment providing physical comfort, emotional climate, psychological needs, and perhaps stimulating sights and sounds. The individual's experiences at this level influence future development in significant ways. Exploration of the experiences of the client as a young child might be valuable in bringing about a successful resolution to treatment issues pertaining to early life events.

FIGURE 4.3. The Star Diagram for the Young Child

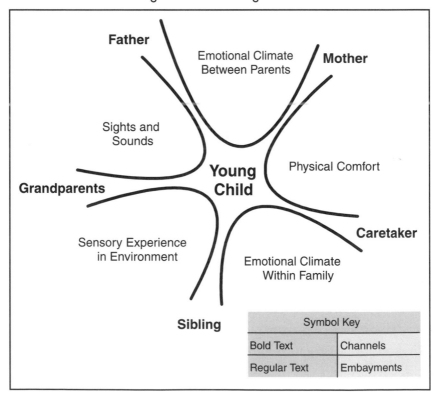

Child

The star diagram for the child would have more channels to significant others, such as siblings, school friends, teachers, and teammates, and more embayments as the environment is more expanded and complex, including school, neighborhood, physical environment, language, religion, cultural influences, and relationships between the parent figures and among family members (see Figure 4.4). Exploration of the more memorable experiences from this stage of life might trigger some helpful insight or provide meaningful information to search for patterns across levels.

Young Adult

The star diagram for the young adult will have expanded. The number and composition of the significant others will probably change a great deal. The number of embayments may increase as the variety of different environments and cultural influences expands to include the broader culture and

FIGURE 4.4. The Star Diagram for the Child

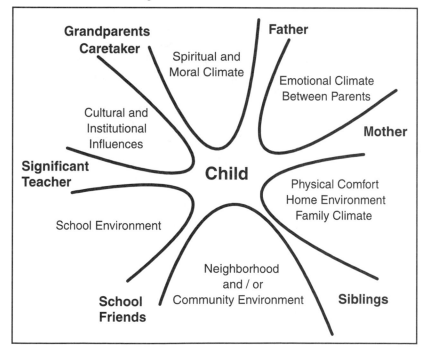

subcultures, exposure to new places and people, new vocational or educational opportunities, and independent living situations (see Figure 4.5). Exploration of present experiences of the young adult or the past experiences of the adult through the analysis of this stage of the community genogram may provide insight into the client's relational patterns.

Adult

Adults may have numerous embayments and channels reflecting the complexities of their lives (see Figure 4.6). They may be between generations, having parents and sometimes grandparents, and their own children and grandchildren. Their work, civic, and social relationships may involve multiple levels and many key individuals and groups. The adult may be struggling to achieve a balance in this multitude of environmental factors that

FIGURE 4.5. The Star Diagram for the Young Adult

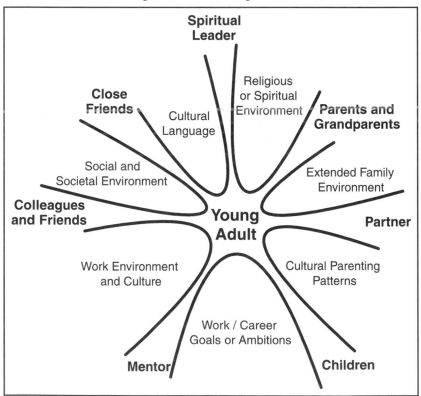

FIGURE 4.6. The Star Diagram for the Adult

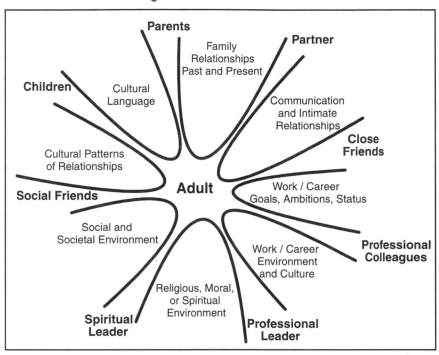

impinge on or promote development and growth. The community genogram can help clients understand the contextual and personal forces influencing their lives.

Senior Adult

While the number of embayments and channels may not be different from the adult star, the nature and key actors that compose the senior adult diagram may be very different (see Figure 4.7). Significant family members and friends are very prominent during this phase. Dependence on others for assistance and medical care may be critical and can be represented in their community genogram. Counselors need to be aware of the client's contextual and cultural interpretations of this stage of life. Often spirituality and mortality are important and particular aspects of their past may be significant for many senior clients.

FIGURE 4.7. The Star Diagram for the Senior Adult

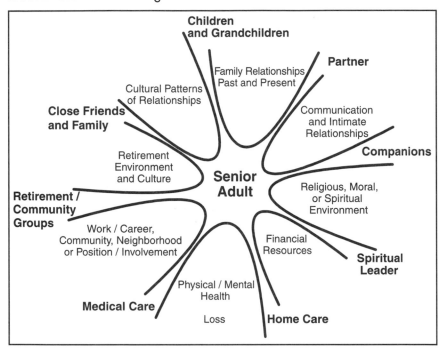

A Life Span Perspective

Several themes are noted when coconstructing individual or relational life span community genograms. For example, it is usually the case that the number of significant environmental influences (i.e., the embayments) increase from early developmental phases to somewhere beyond middle developmental phases. As the number of embayments increase, the impact of any single environmental influence usually diminishes. Additionally, in later developmental phases, the number of environmental influences generally decreases as social and professional contacts are reduced. This decrease also represents the notion that, subsequent to middle developmental phases, individuals and relationships usually have established a sense of stability and integrity so that they are less affected by the larger society or significant others.

Of course, such generalizations cannot be made without noting predominant exceptions. For example, should an individual hold a highly oppressed position within the community, this environmental factor will not easily lose its influential power. Or, should later phases be accompanied by disability or financial distress, environmental factors may still play heavily in self and self-in-relation definition.

A Young Adult Client: The Case of Raj

Raj, a graduate student in psychology, moved from India to undertake doctoral studies at a prestigious university in England. Since his move, he is very much enjoying his new location, friends, mentors, and job. His current community genogram (see Figure 4.8) illustrates his sense that he is going through a major life transition, having to establish his identity in a new position while also spending much time working to complete his dissertation.

Raj participated in a series of interviews that demonstrate the use of a community genogram to integrate similar themes across the life span. During

FIGURE 4.8. An Illustrative Community Genogram: The Case of Raj

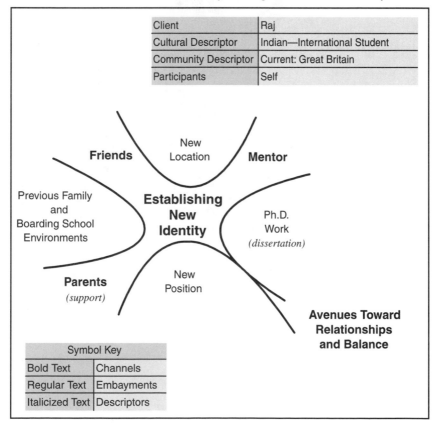

the interviews, Raj recalled a similar time in his life where he was trying to establish his identity while participating in two different environments: his family-of-origin and a private boarding school (see Figure 4.9). The star in the middle of this diagram reflects his emerging identity and the set of parallel dashed lines down the middle of the diagram and around the star itself separate the different environments in which his identity was evolving.

Raj came from a family situation where he experienced much love, support, encouragement, and intellectual stimulation. He remembers feeling very bright and loved being stimulated by ideas and challenges. He spoke about sibling rivalry he experienced with his older sister.

FIGURE 4.9. An Illustrative Community Genogram: Raj as a Child

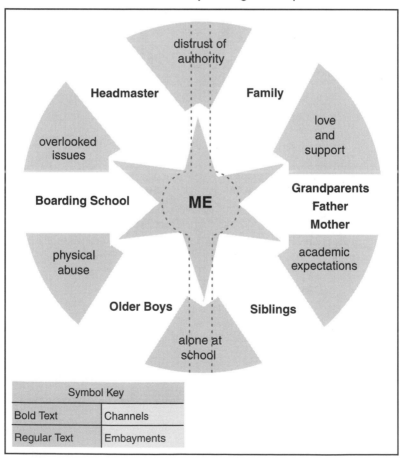

His parents chose to send him to a missionary boarding school that they believed would provide him with a great education. Raj explained that—for his family—being well prepared for advanced education in either medicine or engineering at an early age is key. There is a great deal of pressure to achieve early so that a comfortable status can be maintained.

The boarding school experience significantly changed his life—in a difficult way. As he put it, his life was "going in a wonderful way and then this totally changed that." During these 7 years of his childhood experience, he was made to follow an extraordinarily rigorous schedule and had only a few weeks each year to vacation with his family. He related this experience to his current feelings about routines and pressures and his general tendency to rebel against heavy schedules and early wake-up times.

On the boarding school side of the community genogram, Raj also revealed some experiences of physical abuse, which he never experienced at home. He also experienced some sexual abuse by older male students. One older student in particular was very manipulative and left him powerless. He never told his parents because he didn't want to worry them. There was a need to protect them and a sense that he could take care of this himself. This went on for a while, until Raj finally blew up and yelled at the older manipulative student. Apparently, the headmaster of the school knew about this, but disciplinary action was not taken. The elder boy's high-achiever status allowed the headmaster to turn his head about this inappropriate behavior.

Further on in the interview, Raj noted that there were also some positive parts about the relationship. The older male student could be like an older brother. He took an interest in Raj—because Raj was bright and did not fit in with his peer group—and spent time with him.

After Raj left this school to go to another school, he did a lot of drinking and experimenting with drugs (see Figure 4.10). However, he continued to do well in school and scored high on a national entrance examination that resulted in his acceptance at an engineering school. He never wanted to be an engineer, but there is a sense of very little choice. His father experienced a very difficult time when Raj went into business by himself, instead of going into the family business. This was a way of doing what he would really rather do than his own engineering job.

Raj then applied to a college in England in order to leave India so that he could study what he truly wanted to study, something in the humanities or social sciences, like psychology. This is not valued in India. He would lose significant status and privilege if he studied these subjects. This also would affect whom he could marry. He came to England with his parents' support and encouragement to be what he wants to be—a researcher in the field of experimental psychology.

FIGURE 4.10. An Illustrative Community Genogram: Raj as a Young Adult

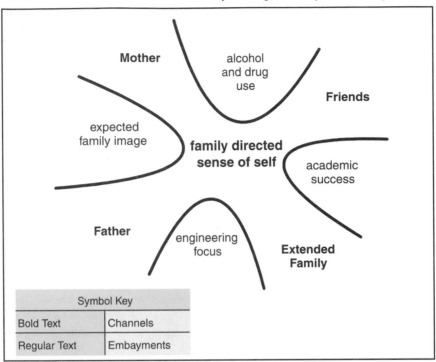

Placing the three star diagrams alongside each other, Raj identified some major themes he was working through. First, Raj realized that his relationship with his family is more important to him now. Although he has not seen his parents for years, he is now more aware of how difficult it must have been for his parents, and especially his mother, to let him go. He is their only son.

Second, as he faces the prospect of his working career, he now is reconsidering a career in academia, particularly academia in England. He wants a more balanced life—not one of staying up all night to get projects done, eating candy bars for dinner, and only focusing on this publication or that data collection. He wants a relationship, a home, and more balance between work and extracurricular activities.

This issue of family ties and balanced work schedules brought up the themes of his loneliness and independence. He was able to identify how in all the community genograms he is alone, and he is still alone at this time in his life. He identifies this as a major focus for the next phase of his life. He is very much in process with understanding his past and how it has affected his choices, and wants to be more cognizant of the choices he makes from this point on.

TAILORING THE COMMUNITY GENOGRAM TO CLIENT NEED

The holistic and flexible composition of the community genogram allows clients to identify and label all the factors that they have deemed important in their lives. Rather than narrowing the historical search to a limited domain, such as family, culture, work, or school experience, the community genogram provides an open forum for clients to choose all the important events and people that have influenced their lives. In therapy, the clinician and client can address the most significant areas to focus on and explore.

Using Multiple Community Genograms

A variety of modifications and extensions to the community genogram are possible, and throughout this book we illustrate numerous formats, depending on client need and therapeutic focus. For example, an individual client could construct three or four of the age-referenced star diagrams to represent different stages of life, including stars about future situations. Patterns across stars could then be explored and major themes about a client's life journey could be identified.

Another example is that the clinician and client coconstruct a "now" star diagram that includes the most important influences and people identified in the client's past and present, and use this to determine how these predominant events and relationships influence the client's current life choices. Still other clients may find value in coconstructing, with significant others, a star diagram for an earlier life phase when a transitional crisis occurred. Future relational star diagrams can present a projected expectation into a later life stage for a client and may identify potential stressful transitions. These examples indicate the versatility community genograms offer for the exploration of the past, present, and future life space of clients.

Modifying the Graphic to Client Need

The form of a community genogram also is open to client discretion. This concept is illustrated throughout the book, and it is essential for clients to feel their community genogram truly reflects their experience. Variation and creativity are welcomed in the process of constructing and interpreting their representations. For example, some clients prefer to be given guidelines and predesigned forms, such as the ones presented thus far in this book. Other clients, however, have expressed interest in creating their own representations. Some highlight geographic information about their community. Others have created more metaphoric images, such as the family floor plan (Coopersmith, 1980), which illustrate relational patterns inside the home as well as where in the community the home is situated. To help deeply understand the client's worldview, a detailed drawing can be very helpful, especially for clients with limited English or verbal communication proficiency. The family floor plan shown in Figure 4.11 is from the Gesili family, who was first introduced in Chapter 2. Again their daughter used the computer to re-create the family floor plan. The dotted line is used to retrace the path she would take when she was in trouble and trying to avoid being spanked. She also recalled being punished and having to sit on the bathroom scale for all her extended family to see. The "plastic" room (where the furniture was usually covered with plastic) was in the front of the house and only used on special occasions. The kitchen faced the back of the house where the block parties were held. Images in the graphics can be realistic or they can be more abstract and geometric in nature. The idea is to use whatever medium will help clients illuminate both the issues that promoted treatment and the potential sources of strength and support that might be tapped in the future.

CONCLUSION: INTERACTIVE ASSESSMENT METHODS AND TREATMENT PLANNING

The method of analysis used to explore a community genogram differs from more standardized instruments (e.g., family genograms) in that clients are encouraged to be creative about how to best represent the important aspects of community influences. Initially, clients are asked to tell stories and relate images and metaphors about what they have included in their community genogram. Allowing for more open and idiosyncratic analysis of the data permits clients to construct their own narratives about the meanings derived from the exploration.

The counselor then facilitates a discussion of the beneficial aspects of the client's experience and assists in a positive asset search before moving toward a negative experience search. Drawing images and personal metaphors from the client about how strengths were used to overcome negative factors provides the client with a deep reservoir of personal resources to call upon to deal with current issues. Specific questioning strategies used to facilitate such dialogues, as well as variations on the basic star format, are provided in the practice sections and case illustrations in each chapter.

FIGURE 4.11. A Computer-Generated Family Floor Plan Variation: The Case of the Gesili Family

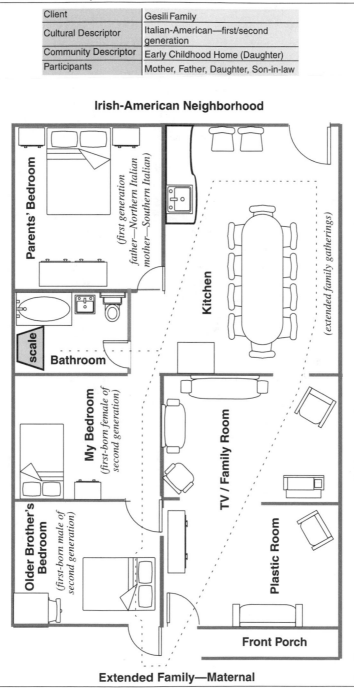

Client	Gesili Family
Cultural Descriptor	Italian-American—first/second generation
Community Descriptor	Early Childhood Home (Daughter)
Participants	Mother, Father, Daughter, Son-in-law

Irish-American Neighborhood

Parents' Bedroom

*(first generation
father—Northern Italian
mother—Southern Italian)*

Kitchen

(extended family gatherings)

Bathroom

scale

My Bedroom

*(first-born female of
second generation)*

TV / Family Room

Older Brother's Bedroom

*(first-born male of
second generation)*

Plastic Room

Front Porch

Extended Family—Maternal

As with the choice of life phases and graphic illustrations, clients should be involved in determining the primary goals and key components of the community genogram. What is important in our community may not be significant to the clients. For one client, religious/spiritual environments, professional work environments, and family relationships may occupy significant embayments. For another, social environments, communication within intimate relationships, and extended family environments may be the identified significant influences. The goal of the community genogram is not to direct clients to deal with prescribed phenomena. Rather, it is to have clients graphically represent those personal, relational, and environmental factors that they feel have had, or continue to have, a profound effect on their lives.

The freedom to choose the specific focus, methods, and goals of exploration permits clients to own the process deeply and therefore lower the contrived aspect of the community genogram. As such, this assessment device can be used in a truly interactive fashion, providing rich information about areas of the multicultural cube deemed important to the clients. From this assessment, clinicians can then begin to tailor treatment to clients, incorporating themes and images raised in the construction and ongoing analysis of the community genogram. This is what is meant by the DCT concept "leading by following." The counselor also is enabled to direct discussion about other areas of the multicultural cube that clients may be less aware of as having a significant influence on their current dilemma.

Clinicians are free to inquire about the quality and implications of the relationships identified in the community genogram as well as to wonder about relationships that are not graphically represented. We believe that the client and the counselor both play a role in the coconstruction of narratives that flow through the community genogram, but that it is ultimately the client that establishes the significance or importance of the relationship. As counselors, we cannot give clients insights into their issues. Instead, we can join in conversations with them about their life, and we can pose questions and highlight patterns as we see them. However, it is only when clients internalize this information as their own that they are able to use it to make changes in their lives. The community genogram provides a field for clients to begin the process of validating, examining, and transforming their own beliefs about the significant relationships in their lives. In the next chapter an in-depth analysis of one client's community genogram will demonstrate how to surface and examine deep-seated beliefs that were inculcated in her community-of-origin.

CHAPTER 5

Contextualizing the Self in Counseling and Therapy

This chapter highlights the intensive exploration that is possible from an individual community genogram within the limitations of one session. The case study that comprises most of the chapter demonstrates a set of questioning strategies used by the clinician to extend the client's worldview concerning the issues promoting treatment. In this regard, the community genogram, along with skillful questioning strategies, can be used to help uncover, work through, enhance, expand, deconstruct, and reconstruct the narratives clients can then use to maximize the therapeutic benefits of counseling and therapy.

Several aspects of treatment are discussed in this chapter:

- **How to introduce and use the community genogram in individual treatment settings**
- **How to use a coconstructive process (matching then leading by following)**
- **How to help clients see themselves-in-relation**
- **How to use the cultural identity theory to track client locus of concern**
- **How to explore issues of boundaries and power in a client's community genogram**
- **How to use questioning strategies to bring out client narrative**

Social constructivism sets the foundation for work with all interactive assessment devices. Having our clients generate the meaning from their lives, as opposed to the therapist making interpretations about client stories is at the basis of this shift in therapeutic work. Our emphasis needs to be on the meaning that develops in the ongoing narratives developed by clients and clinicians. The personal meanings and interpersonal contexts that emerge in counseling need to be our primary concern. It is through the counseling relationship that this forum for change is created (Gergen, 1999; Mahoney, 2003; Sexton & Whiston, 1994).

Coconstructivist counseling practice shares the postmodern belief in the rejection of the concept of one ultimate truth. Thus the process of assessment and the categorization of dysfunction do not rely on the use of absolute external criteria, but rather rely on the subjective and relative criteria used by the client (Neimeyer & Raskin, 2000). As Hayes (1994) notes, in reconstructing the past, the client serves as his or her own historian, which suggests the superimposition of a present context over the past. Thus client narratives may be seen more as fabrication than as a re-creation (Howard, 1991).

Client narrative is facilitated through focused questioning strategies intended to uncover the client's construction of meaning. Through this narrative format, coconstructivist counselors will want to focus more on present understandings in the service of future actions than on past action in the service of present understandings. In this case study, notice how the client and counselor use the community genogram to re-story the client narrative to surface strengths and emerging resources.

SETTING A SAFE AND ENABLING CONTEXT FOR TREATMENT

Preparing clients to participate and create a community genogram is an important first step. Most clients will not be familiar with community genograms and may need specific directions or examples to follow. The directions noted at the end of Chapter 2 can be used to help guide clients in developing their community genogram. Another way to introduce this strategy might be to share your own community genogram that emphasizes your professional development or key relationships and experiences from your past. This will not only demonstrate what a community genogram looks like, it will also expedite the joining process. Sample community genograms, like those in this book, can be shared to "cast the net open" to see which client issues surface, or these can be used to zero-in on issues you and the client identify as needing more exploration.

The coconstructive position we advocate attempts to rebalance the power relationship between client and clinician. One concrete signal of this more equalitarian relationship is to jointly design and select the specific questions that will be used to explore the community genogram. Together, clients and practitioners enter into a joint exploration where no "surprise" questions will be used to make the client uncomfortable. This is not to say that in the spontaneity of the examination, new questions that arise cannot be entertained. The point we are stressing is to ask clients if they are ready to delve into this area before we move in that direction. By sharing the questions beforehand and getting agreement before pursuing evolving issues, we communicate that this process is shared and that both client and counselor will be involved in the decision-making process. Keep in mind that the goal of postmodern therapeutic interventions is to enable clients to develop more adaptable and viable personal constructions rather than the elimination and revision of cognitive distortions or corrective emotional experiences (Neimeyer & Harter, 1988).

USING COMMUNITY GENOGRAMS IN TREATMENT: ILLUSTRATIVE DIALOGUES

In the dialogues that follow throughout this chapter, key features of a coconstructive approach from the beginning to the end of one session are presented. We have chosen to use an annotated transcript approach to illustrate how the community genogram can be incorporated into counseling. Our comments are interspersed throughout the transcriptions and are enclosed in brackets.

The questions and activities demonstrated here are typical of the kind that may be used in one session or over a larger number of counseling sessions. Our purpose is to relate the flow of therapeutic dialogue generated by the community genogram to essential coconstructive counseling concepts. The case begins in the third session of individual counseling. The client, Magdalena, is a 40-year-old Chamorro female.

Identifying Salient Issues

Therapist: I do have the questions that we may be exploring. And I've talked to you about them already. What are your thoughts about this?

[Therapist shares questions beforehand to ensure maximum client input.]

Client: I think it's really helpful in providing me with a sense of purpose and knowing that this is going to be okay. So it provides a sense of safety, because I know what to expect. And I feel that there aren't going to be any surprises. So that's real helpful to me.

[Client expresses safety and control.]

Therapist: And to structure this, I would like first of all just to ask about the general issue you'd like to talk about. But we're not going to go into that in any particular depth in the beginning. We're just going to outline the general issue. Then we'll move to a community genogram. We're looking for some cultural and family supports before we go and deal with the issue itself.

[Therapist provides overview of how to approach issues—start with general and work toward specifics. Thus further reassurance is conveyed to client about the exploration process.]

Initiating Questions

Getting clients to express their own ideas about their issues represented in their community genogram is an important first step toward constructive narrative treatment. Providing questions that are as open-ended as possible is a good place to begin. Be careful not to use language in your questions that pushes the client to consider the issues from a particular perspective. For example, "How do you define the *problem*?" places a negative connotation on the issues and puts both client and clinician in a judgmental position.

Questions that target a specific type of response are equally nonproductive when used at the beginning of treatment: "Tell me how you *feel*." "What are your *thoughts* at this time?" "What are the *behaviors* you would most like to change?" Questions such as these limit our clients' responses to affective, cognitive, or behavioral levels and may not provide sufficient latitude for them to identify and describe their own focus of concerns.

Specific questions, focused at particular ways of experiencing and interpreting the world will be important at later stages of the exploration process, but at the beginning these questions do not permit the client to establish the working language and constructions that *we will follow* throughout treatment.

We have found the following questioning format useful at the beginning of treatment:

- "Could you tell what you wanted to share today?"
- "When you focus on your community genogram, what are you aware of?"
- "What happened for you as you constructed the community genogram?"

These types of questions allow for the personal constructions of clients to come forth, providing a broad overview of their reactions to making the community genogram. These reactions and insights, triggered by the construction process, give us information about where on the multicultural cube (see Figure 4.2) the client is focusing.

Therapist: Could you tell what you wanted to share today?
Client: I think what I was looking at was how people don't necessarily— there's a general ignorance about Chamorros that I find disturbing, particularly since we have been part of the United States for some

time. And that general sense of ignorance is quite pervasive. So in a way it negates our uniqueness as well as our place as people.

[The client's narrative could be placed at the group level for locus of treatment and is bringing up multicultural issues of ethnicity and race. The client is discussing her issues from a formal orientation, using conceptual language, particularly noticeable in the last sentence.]

Therapist: So you feel your people's place has been neglected and denied?

[Therapist paraphrases central feelings and presents a question that focuses from the group's (Chamorro) to her own experiences.]

Client: Yes.

Therapist: How has it been for you personally?

Client: At different stages of my development, I think I've had different emotions and different thoughts about it. I'm at a stage where I'm looking at being proactive and saying, "Okay, people aren't necessarily responsible, because society is such that if the numbers of people aren't high enough (population size), people just don't care." You just somehow are subsumed into a much larger group. And in a sense, neglected.

[The client continues to use a formal, reflective orientation ("at different stages") and places the issue of neglect within a societal background.]

Therapist: Now, one of the things I'm hearing is that you really already are beginning to see yourself as a person in cultural context. So you start with a very high level of consciousness of yourself as a Chamorro and what that means to you. Is that correct?

[Therapist is able to hear that the client is operating at the reflective level and communicates this to the client for confirmation.]

Client: As I am today. Yes.

Introducing the Community Genogram

From this brief introduction the client has shared sufficient information for the therapist to begin formulating a map to use in exploring the community genogram. Client issues of oppression, her strong identification with her ethnic group, and her formal worldview must be addressed as the exploration moves further. In a sense, the client has constructed the map the therapist is now going to follow. Figure 5.1 presents Magdalena's community genogram.

FIGURE 5.1. An Illustrative Community Genogram: The Case of Magdalena

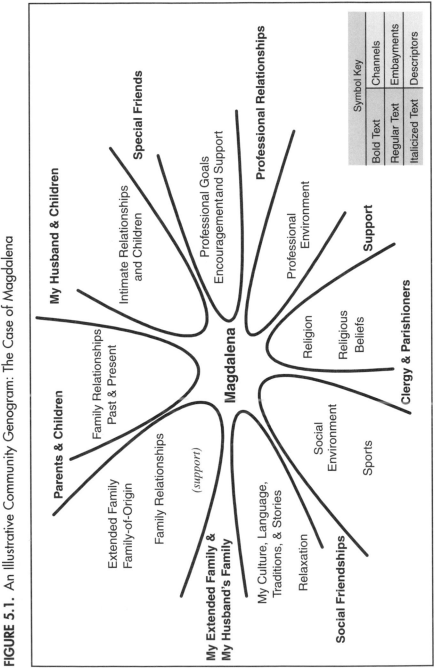

Therapist: The way I'd like to begin exploring the cultural context is to have you talk me through your community genogram. Could you tell me what is here in your story that you represented in this community genogram?

Client: As I am today?

Therapist: As you are today.

[The therapist prompts the client to begin the exploration of the community genogram in a very open-ended fashion. This allows the client to identify key images and story lines represented in the genogram.]

Client: So I'm looking at the left outside, or the peak—the structures or systems that are most important to me. So there's my parents and siblings. My husband, Felix, and my children, Alison and Aaron. Then special friends.

Therapist: Mmm-hmm.

[Staying in the "present," the client begins with her most important support systems.]

Client: Coming over here to the extended family. And that includes my family through Felix, social friends, religion. And professional relationships. And each of those things—each of those systems— provide a different sense of support or different way of being. But I think all of it represents who I am. In family relations. Relationships. That support—family relationships, past and present—intimate relationships, professional, and so forth. I think, in terms of the extended family and social friends, it's culture, language, tradition, stories, relaxation, and religion would be traditions and beliefs.

[As the client shares information about the other key support systems, she reinforces their interconnectedness ("I think all of it represents who I am"). She is signifying the importance she places on the connection between culture, community, family, and self. Her sense of self-in-relation is now heightened by this initial overview of her community genogram.]

Connecting Culture to Self

A central aim of the analysis of a community genogram is to help clients relate their current situation to their ethnic heritage and background. Helping clients realize that they are a part of a wider (cultural) movement can be very reassuring. It not only provides a contextual backdrop to re-story the present life script, but it opens up avenues to potential resources that might be overlooked. Focusing clients on cultural traditions and symbols is one way to help them see the connection between culture and themselves.

Therapist: I would like to continue your discussion of the Chamorros— could we focus a little bit here on the culture, language, and traditions? How did Chamorro culture affect you growing up?

[Casting the net wide, the therapist asks for any connections the client can see between cultural heritage and her development.]

Client: When I think about Chamorro culture . . . I really think of the extended family [she points to the left side of the community genogram]. And what comes to mind is images of spending time at my uncle's ranch. And it wasn't just my brothers and myself; it was my extended family, including cousins, aunts, and uncles. We would always get together. And this image of all the children just running up the hills, of picking guavas. It was a real exciting, warm, safe environment because we didn't have just one parent; we had a lot of parents. And there was a lot of care going around.

[The same theme—extended family and strong support—is identified by the client.]

Therapist: So this image that you have—you and the children running up the hill to pick guavas. That's a feeling that many parents, many people, many caretakers—are very important to you.

[Images are specific illustrations of a person's story. They provide details about events that punctuate the client's recollections. The feelings associated with these images will be important touchstones to revisit throughout the entire course of therapy. By paraphrasing, the therapist connotes the importance of these images for the client and participates in the coconstruction process.]

Client: Mmm-hmm.
Therapist: Could you share more about your Chamorro culture?

[This question asks for further elaboration about the client's perceptions about her culture.]

Client: Okay. Chamorros are the people of Guam. They're also the people from the Marianas Islands. Guam is the largest island in the Marianas chain. But there are other Chamarros. They are people from Saipan, Rota or Luta, Tinian, and other smaller islands. But we have a history and a language and traditions and belief systems that continue to bind us over the years. Although political changes have occurred that somehow separated us from the other islands, we are still very much Chamorros.

[Oftentimes, clients will begin with historical accounts and specific geographical information about their ethnic group. This information helps create a mutual understanding between client and therapist about significant cultural events.]

Therapist: "We are very much Chamorros." I heard some strength in you as you said that.
Client: Mmm-hmm.
Therapist: What are some images that come to your mind as you imagine being a Chamorro?

[The therapist highlights the theme of family strength before asking for some more specific images.]

Client: Images of sitting with large families. The elderly people, the grandparents, the aunts and uncles. There's a high sense of respect for them. Warmth around food, sharing, generosity, caring, supporting one another. Those are the types of characteristics that come to mind when I think about what it means to be Chamorro.

[A clear cultural theme emerges, consistent with the extended family images the client has already shared. These images further reinforce the link between culture and family for this client. Again, sensations and descriptions focus on warmth, support, and caring communicated through the extended family.]

Therapist: So it's that extended family that really catches the meaning of being Chamorro for you?
Client: Yes.

[The therapist begins anchoring cultural strengths to the client, establishing the potential for future access.]

Intensifying the Positive Asset Search

While cultural and family contexts provide a backdrop for conducting a positive asset search (Ivey et al., 2002), it is only the strengths to which a client has direct access that can be used to initiate the change process. Asking clients to use the strength of their ancestors to overcome their present issues is a little too abstract. Clients need to know that they themselves have the power and the resources to work through their current problems. The contextual information is essential in that it acts as an amplification of the personal strengths identified by the client. In this stage of the community genogram analysis, the focus moves to the identification and intensification of specific images of client strength. Here is one example of a positive asset search.

Therapist: I would like to go back to your view of yourself with your family, your extended family; what central image comes to your mind in relationship to that extended family?

[The question seeks a core image that will resonate with the client's personal experience.]

Client: It's hard for me to think of one image, because there's so many images where there's support, and reciprocity, and a general caring. The image that comes to mind most readily is the image of a lot of people. And you're not all from the same nuclear family. And there's this connection that we have with one another—that distance doesn't separate us—it's images around kitchens, eating, talking, people dropping in. So that image of always—that openness—is what I find as being very important.

[For this client, the recurrent image of many people sharing support and care continues. Strong bonds that permit closeness and openness are the key images in this passage.]

Therapist: So the closeness and openness. Please take that image again of closeness and openness and imagine one of those times. And then just sort of see it in your mind's eye for just a moment. What are you seeing?

[The therapist begins to have the client personalize these images. Clear, detailed, and specific images help intensify the feelings associated with these strengths.]

Client: Just a lot of people hugging, laughing, talking, eating. There's a lot of touching. They're just images of warmth and support.
Therapist: And as you get these images . . . what feelings flow through you?

[These statements reflect more sensorimotor processing by this client and the therapist wonders about the affective dimension of these images.]

Client: It's a sense of safety and warmth. And—and just—just goes right through me.
Therapist: Can you locate that feeling of safety and warmth in your body?
Client: Right here [gestures to her torso].
Therapist: Right here. So that Chamorro safety and warmth, basically, is always with you, anytime you want to call on that image.

[The physicality of these sensations is important. For the first time in the interview, the feelings and sensations the client is experiencing are directly connected to the cultural strengths identified in early stages of the community genogram analysis. Through the use of images the strengths are anchored to the body.]

Expressing the Negative Story

By building a sufficient reservoir of cultural, community, family, and personal strength, the focus of the analysis is now ready to shift to the issues that prompted treatment. Although many clients may want to begin with the negative stories contained in the configurations of their community genogram, it is essential that a base of strength be established prior to delving into the painful parts of the client's life script. With a positive foundation, clients are better able to face their problems or concerns and will have more psychic energy to participate in a re-storying process that can identify potential solutions.

Our case picks up after a positive asset search identified "resiliency" as another resource the client could access from her cultural experience. The next transcription illustrates how to use the community genogram to locate and analyze constraining forces operating within the life space of our clients.

Therapist: I know we've looked at what you originally came to talk about very briefly. And I'd like to return to that, and we've always got those resources of resiliency, warmth, support, and caring available to you. You were talking about the whole issue of sometimes your people are not recognized, and you are not recognized. I'd kind of like to hear some more specific stories of what occurred there and what you saw, heard, felt. Could you tell me one of the stories?

[The therapist summarizes the strengths identified thus far and sets the stage to begin the analysis of negative stories. Asking for specific details of the stories helps center clients in the experience.]

Client: When I was in eighth grade, and I had this civics teacher who, you know, had a full classroom. And the civics teacher had this attitude, and we were—in our culture, you don't—you were supposed to respect the teacher. Well, this teacher had just gotten into this mode of telling us how we were—or how Chamorros were—ignorant. We were lazy. We were not going to get anywhere, in many, many different words. After a while, it just all came down to this almost hatred or dislike for us.

[The client quickly begins describing this experience she had in school. It is reflective of the encounter phase of cultural identity and it had a profound effect on her life. The roots of discrimination can often be traced back to specific events that happen in a client's life.]

> And this was a contract teacher who was brought from the mainland to Guam. And I was really angry about what he was saying. And I was also very angry about what was happening, which was because of our belief that we are not—or our rule that you don't speak against authority—everybody just sat there. But as this man went on and on and on, I just got angrier and angrier. And this lack of respect just really hit me. And I just broke my pencil and threw it on the ground and said some obscenity and walked out.

[The teacher was asking students to act in a way that was inconsistent with cultural expectations.]

Therapist: And what was the upshot of that?

Client: Of course I was very upset. And afterwards, he came up to me and he said that I got an A. And I said, "Why?" You know. And I was still very angry. And he said, "Because you reacted. You got angry." And so I was even angrier about that. Because how about all of the other people who were going to obey the rule and continue to be angry in silence?

[The teacher placed the client in a double bind. By breaking her cultural norms she succeeded in this school-related task. She felt very bad about the other students who did not break the norm but remained silent and did not get As. This conflictual situation made a powerful mark on her life.]

> And he wasn't really thinking about our culture and how what I did was very wrong in my culture. And what he wanted me to do— you know, so—there were two cultures clashing. It just wasn't something that was appropriate in our culture.
>
> So this was the upshot. I could understand why he was doing that, but I think his style was very degrading. I think what he wanted to do was get us to react and get excited about school, but what he did do was turn people very much against education or school, or what we call *Haoles*—Caucasians or people from—outsiders. So instead of helping us to feel empowered, he tried to disempower us. And that really upset me.

[Although she could understand the teacher's rationale, she was still able to see the cultural insensitivity of this type of learning situation. The difference in power between the teacher and student is clearly highlighted in this exchange.]

[Here the client has moved to the naming phase of cultural identity. Names for outsiders and the use of the term *disempower*, plus the intense anger associated with this encounter, are all indicative of the naming phase.]

Therapist: It's one of these really foundational incidents where I can tell you feel a lot of power in that, still.

Client: Mmm-hmm. It still comes back to me. And I think I see it being done by teachers in different ways, but it's basically the same thing. It's somehow by humiliating or degrading someone who is poor or who is from a different culture, somehow the teacher feels more empowered and so—I respond to that because it's—I can identify with those children.

[The client also generalizes her experience to that of other students, and she sees the disempowerment that still plays out in schoolrooms in her country and in the United States.]

Therapist: I can sense that anger. Where do you feel that anger in your body?

Client: Oh, just right here. It's just all over. Right here [voice is trembling].

[Feelings associated with negative stories are also anchored in the body and helping clients identify and express those emotions can be very therapeutic.]

Therapist: Such disrespect. Could we just hang onto that for a minute and go back to that image of the family and the connectedness and the caring and that resiliency?

Client: [sigh]

Therapist: What's happening for you right now?

Client: It's really hard shifting. But I feel a lot better. I try to think about my parents and my aunts. But I guess the feeling of frustration is very much there.

[By bringing forward the positive strengths identified in the first part of the community genogram analysis, the client is able to receive some small sense of relief.]

Moving Toward the Reflective Consciousness

The comprehensive analysis of the community genogram assists clients in identifying the major themes that have influenced their lives to date. They are enabled to examine these themes and to explore specific examples of how the themes were played out in particular situations. The emotions, details, and patterns associated with these examples set the stage to coconstruct a re-storying of the client's narrative. By helping clients think back about their stories and relating these experiences to present, we can discuss how they would like their lives to be different in the future. The real power to change is engendered by the exploration of past stories in light of the present to improve what's about to happen next. In this next excerpt, the therapist helps the client regain a lost sense of power by asking her to focus on the past story, but from a present perspective.

Therapist: At this moment, I'd like to ask the most general question as you reflect back upon the stories: What stands out for you and what occurs for you?

[The therapist uses the recollections of the past to search for patterns and themes. The focus is on the present observing the past.]

Client: What occurs to me is . . . the ignorance and the lack of respect that is going to be present. It'll be until I'm gone and after I'm gone because it's just a part of people. People will—maybe not intentionally, but unintentionally—affect others the same way. So that's what stands out for me, is that, you know, just primarily ignorance and unintentional racism or oppression. I don't know.

[Often clients may "excuse" those who have inflicted oppression in the past. This is a form of psychological distancing (denial, rationalization) that delays and can even interfere with the integration of a more positive stance about the realities of living in an oppressive environment.]

Therapist: Or sometimes even intentional.
Client: Sometimes intentional. But it's going to be there.
Therapist: So racism and oppression are going to be there.

[Here the therapist focuses on intentional as well as unintentional oppression.]

Client: Right.
Therapist: [sigh] Now, given that, thinking back for a moment about your teacher, what could you tell me about your teacher? What was going on for him?

[This question moves the client from a general reflection to examine in-depth the situation with her teacher from a new perspective. This shift in focus is aimed at helping the client coconstruct multiperspectives and achieve internalization about this crucial episode.]

Client: Well, I think I never really spoke to him and asked him what was going on for him. But what I, you know, reflecting back to what it must have been like for him, he was far away from home. Very far away from home. In a place that the culture's very different. Somehow he was on a mission to help us. And he might have tried different ways of doing it. And I'm speaking as a teacher. Teachers try different strategies. And I think it's like, the overall frustration of how you communicate certain things to people. You really don't know.

Later, on toward the end of the year, he had hikes. He would invite students to go on hikes in different parts of the island, and that was the different side of him, outside of the classroom. He was extending and sharing on something he enjoyed, and making it possible for us to go out. So I could see that he was trying to adjust as well as find a way to connect with us. And the outdoors seemed to work well for him. So I think he—when I look back—he was just trying to figure out, "How do I reach the students?" when we are really taught to not speak out.

[The client is able to bring her professional experience as a teacher to bear on this re-storying process. Placing the traumatic experience in the classroom as one strategy, the client is able to reassess the situation in light of decisions and goals. These recollections now bring out the larger context of the situation. The client is able to see other ways this teacher tried to reach out to the students.]

Therapist: How was it for you as—what you said at that time—for you, as a student at that younger age, how was it for you? How did you experience it at that time, as you reflect on it now?

[These questions assist in the re-storying process. By looking at the past through our present we are able to recast the players and the context to extract the personal strengths and cultural resources embedded in the re-storying process.]

Client: I think . . .
Therapist: You're an older person now looking back at that time.
Client: Uh-huh. When I think about back at that time, you know, seventh grade was just a haze. It's like I could have been sleeping. [small laugh] But eighth grade, I think I started to become more aware of my surroundings, the people that were in the classes, the social environment, as well as how I was doing in school. Looking at being involved in different things. So I was not so much self-centered. I was becoming a lot more, you know, moving out—outward. And to hear this from someone who I'm supposed to respect . . .

[In this client passage, more specificity about her own developmental journey is provided. These personal issues are important for the fuller understanding of the situation, but notice that they do not absolve the teacher of being culturally inappropriate.]

Therapist: Yeah?

Client: Really took me aback. But I guess, if I'm looking at the transition developmentally, I felt that that was probably appropriate, given that I didn't have other avenues or outlets. You know, I couldn't go to a counselor, for example, and say, you know, "This teacher is really giving me a hard time," or "You should hear what he's saying," because that still isn't appropriate. You have to imagine that, in the school, the teacher is the source of knowledge and power.

[Her hurt and disappointment are still evident. Here the client is clarifying that no other resources were available to help her work through the issues at that time.]

Therapist: Mmm-hmm. You say it still is inappropriate.

[The therapist has the client shift to another example.]

Client: I can remember being at the university level and a French teacher being very upset because she would raise a question and nobody would say anything . . . it's that it was to call attention to oneself is considered inappropriate. To say "Yes, I know the answer" is also inappropriate. I guess you're not supposed to share the limelight. But I've come a long way. In classes here I feel very comfortable [speaking up] because I feel that it's the next step. I can no longer sit back because then I also limit my learning.

[Here the client acknowledges how she has shifted in her understanding of the teacher-student relationship so that she may maximize the benefits from a learning opportunity.]

Shifting from Reflective Consciousness to Internalization

Helping our clients retrace significant events provides specific issues that can be examined under the framework of the cultural identity theory. Using the community genogram as a focal point and a backdrop, clients are enabled to tell their stories of oppression and trauma. In the previous stage of analysis (reflective consciousness) the client was asked to reassess her recollections in light of who she is today. This reevaluation often provides a temporal distance that provides an opportunity for the development of new perspectives on that critical situation. In this final stage of the re-storying process, the client is assisted to coconstruct a multiperspective integration of the cultural, personal, and situational factors that influence the initial experience. This internalization stance is used to facilitate a positive integration of the past and to guide future action. Only when clients can accept the past can they feel empowered to handle the future. Our case resumes as the therapist points out the double bind the client finds herself in as she moves into non-Chamorro cultures.

Therapist: But nonetheless, the whole idea of challenging and so forth doesn't really feel personally or culturally comfortable to you at all—good—frequently. Is that right?

Client: Right.

Therapist: Actually, then, going ahead and challenging this guy or the teacher here would really be a violation of your cultural idea of respect, wouldn't it?

Client: Right.

Therapist: But you're in a double bind.

[Many of our clients' issues are really culturally related and we need to help them reexamine both the cultural implications as well as the actions of themselves and others in the re-storying process.]

Client: Mmm-hmm. But in a sense that when you go back to the community genogram we have talked about cultural shifts. In a sense, I was really raised in a bicultural environment, because the shifts were already made, when they started saying you couldn't speak, you know, our language in school. Bad, bad, bad. What was being taught was not just the language—the English language—it was the American values. So there's a real dichotomy that goes on, I think, for most Chamorros. And identity, who are we? And where do we go from here? And how do we succeed, you know, in this society that we're—we have to be a part of, and that we are a part of? So, for example, talking in class is uncomfortable in Guam because our peers would be looking at me, and "Oh, look at her. Who does she think she is?" But here, it's—you know, I don't have that kind of pressure or perceptions placed upon me.

[In this passage the client recounts the history and examines the major questions that are left for her people as they [she] struggle with identity issues.]

Therapist: So how do you make sense of this?

Client: You have to remember, I was raised with two values. Not necessarily congruent. Not necessarily the same. And I think what allows me to be successful in both cultures is that I can shift. And I can acknowledge the strengths of the values of both cultures or both societies. I think the hardest part is when a person can't shift. Or is stuck. And then becomes successful in only one area in one culture.

[Here the client is capturing the double bind she feels. From this awareness a new understanding is beginning to develop. The integration of the two cultures is becoming more evident. The multiperspective integration is very obvious. Her statements reinforce the multiple options available within a bicultural context. The sharp boundaries that existed between cultures at the start of the session are now blurring and a positive internalization is emerging.]

Therapist: What would you like to do about some of your knowledge and awareness? How can we work together, perhaps even to take some action for the young people, young Chamorro people?

[The question emphasizes the translation of awareness into action. The therapist implicitly indicates his availability to assist in this process.]

Client: Really extending myself as opposed to being passive, becoming more active. Collaborating with others to pursue areas of interest that would help both cultures, both on Guam and out here [United States]. Speaking out and just being active, doing something about it, is what I see as helpful. Presenting the image to young Chamorros that there's—there is pride in being Chamorro and there's pride in being an American. And you don't have to be one or the other because we've evolved and taken what I think is valuable in both cultures and—to become who we are.

[While these statements are general, they indicate a heightened sense of integration and are really the beginning steps toward action. The renewed understanding that she is a member of both cultures has enabled her to coalesce her ideas and to present a cogent and salient message to others in similar situations. Specific actions, based on this motivating concept, will follow.]

Therapist: And so, then, in back of your community genogram, there really is a real history—not just Chamorro—but American pride that you have as well?
Client: Oh, yes!

[The significance of the community genogram is reinforced.]

CONCLUSION: CLIENT MEANING MAKING AND THE COMMUNITY GENOGRAM

The case study of Magdalena illustrates the efficacy of using the community genogram to assist clients in drawing meaningful links between their past, present, and future. The power of the community genogram lies in the fact that clients have control over what they include in the graphic, that they are the major authors of the re-storying process during the session, and that they can quickly and graphically see the connections between and among disparate events and situations by referring to the genogram. By increasing clients' control over content, interpretation, and connections, meaning is enhanced. They are able to discuss topics that are important to them and see links to other situations and developmental issues that help demonstrate continuity and change. The analysis of the community genogram helps them move from the familiar perspectives that offer limited resources to new perspectives that open a wide array of options to guide enlightened points of view and actions.

The community genogram is a record of their lives, and they can examine that record in numerous ways. The questioning strategy followed by the therapist in this case study was aimed at moving the client along the cultural awareness continuum. Although the client presented interesting issues of cultural imperialism, any traumatic or oppressive issues could have been examined in the same way. Client meaning is enhanced by the storytelling nature of this process. Specific examples, followed by an illumination of themes or patterns, leading to new insights and actions is a common therapeutic formula used to liberate the client's personal and cultural resources. The community genogram adds a new dimension to this therapeutic dialogue by bringing in visual material that can be easily retrieved to make connections, to see patterns, and to understand themes. The concrete and visual nature of the community genogram deepens the analytic process inherent in most counseling and therapy sessions.

CHAPTER 6

Using Community Genograms with Families: A Coconstructivist Perspective

This chapter demonstrates how to use the community genogram within a systemic approach to counseling and therapy. Covering the major phases of the therapeutic encounter, this chapter illustrates the value of augmenting clinical information gathered through traditional intake and assessment methods with the situated knowledge gained from the analysis of the community genogram. The systemic and contextual aspects of the community genogram are highlighted as ways to stimulate discussion, exploration, enhancement, and transformation of intrafamilial and extrafamilial relationships. As a graphic tool, the community genogram can be used in conjunction with any version of systemic treatment. In this chapter, a coconstructive lens is used to examine how to use a community genogram within a format of couples therapy.

Five major points are emphasized in this chapter:

- **The definition of coconstructivism**
- **How to introduce and use the community genogram in relational treatment settings**
- **How to use a coconstructive process in family therapy**
- **How to help clients see themselves-in-relationship within their nuclear and extended family and community networks**
- **How to explore issues of cohesiveness and hierarchy in a family's community genogram**

DEFINING COCONSTRUCTIVISM

Coconstructivism is one of many postmodern approaches that place value on the role of social constructions in how counselors formulate and work with clients. Individual and family counseling methods emerging from a postmodern perspective represent an important alternative to traditional counseling practice. The major difference is that traditional counseling methods assume a single, consistent, and recognizable reality that exists independent from the knower; alternative, postmodern perspectives suggest the existence of multiple realities derived from interactions between the knower and the environment that are mediated by individual, family, social, cultural, and temporal factors (see Figure 1.1). This is true for the client and the mental health professional. Thus reality is viewed as relative and changeable; a function of both personal and social constructions (Mahoney, 2003).

Accordingly, while traditional approaches view clients and client systems as nonadaptive reactors to a known environment and aim to help them adapt to this environment, postmodern approaches view clients as active agents within the environment and seek to extend their capabilities beyond intrapersonal, interactional, and sociocultural constraints. Postmodern approaches reject the tendency to pathologize idiosyncratic differences that emerge across our spectrum of clients when the primary focus of the therapist is a treatment plan designed to ameliorate dysfunction assumed to reside within clients. Postmodern approaches instead advance a multidimensional, nonpathological, and contextually based form of practice illuminating the many forces that contribute to the notion of disorder and growth (Rigazio-DiGilio, Ivey, & Locke, 1997). Because understanding the social context is an essential aspect of postmodern treatment, the community genogram is an ideal tool to help clients work through the multiple mazes of their social situations.

DIFFERENTIATING POSTMODERN COUNSELING THEORIES

Not all postmodern counseling methods are coconstructive. In fact, three distinct variations have been identified in the field: constructivism, social constructionism, and coconstructivism. The three branches draw from one another, yet each can be distinguished by its unique focal points of treatment (i.e., intrapsychic, interactional, contextual). The community genogram can be used with all three frameworks but is particularly helpful within the contextually based process associated with coconstructivist methods. To clarify the coconstructive value of the community genogram, a brief differentiation of the three forms of postmodern counseling are presented before illustrating how to use the community genogram in conjunction with coconstructive family counseling.

Constructivist Perspectives

Constructivist theories emphasize an intrapsychic perspective on the nature of self, and focus on internal processes of self-construction, giving less attention to the social contexts influencing individual physiology, cognitive functioning, and systemic meaning making. Radical formulations based on *ontological realism* define reality as a subjective phenomenon that exists as an extension of the knower (Maturana & Varela, 1987; Von Foerster, 1984; Von Glaserfeld, 1991; Watzlawick, 1984). Less radical formulations based on *hypothetical realism* posit that we live in an unknowable, but nonetheless inescapable, world that can enhance or constrain our ability to be self-sufficient creators of our experience (see Guidano, 1995; Howard, 1991; Kelly, 1955; Mahoney, 2003; Polkinghorne, 1994). Constructivism focuses on the process of self-construction used to define a sense of self, self-in-relation, and environment, and asserts, with varying conditions of exception, the capacity of individuals to extend beyond constraining and oppressive constructions toward multiple perspectives and possibilities.

Social Constructionist Perspectives

Social constructionist theories represent variations within an interactive perspective that emphasize social meaning-making processes (Berger & Luckmann, 1966; Burr, 1995; Hayes, 1994). These theories assert that the constructions we formulate about ourselves and the world emerge from linguistic constructions maintained and perpetuated in the domain of intersubjective conversation (Guterman, 1994) and represent socially constructed concepts that are subject to change depending upon the social-cultural-historical context in which one lives (D'Andrea, 2000). As such, primary attention is given to understanding the characteristics of the cultural and contextual environment that contains the language systems that clients use to define the self and their sense of self-in-relation.

Social constructionists seek to assist clients to extend beyond the narratives of the dominant culture that constrain individual, interrelational, and cultural possibilities (Anderson & Goolishian, 1988; Brown, 2000; Daniels & White, 1994; Dell, 1982; Gergen, 1999; Hoffman, 1990; Keeney, 1983; White, 1995). For example, the terms we use to define ourselves are derived from the dominant or local culture. Certain terms and images of ourselves are intended to limit our possibilities. Terms that infer segregation, exclusion, stereotypes, and inferiority are used by the dominant culture to minimize the power of certain groups while maximizing the self-interests of other groups. The debate about gay and lesbian marriage reflects how language is used—on both sides of the issue—to classify individuals and to influence the discussion toward a desired outcome. Within the social constructionist perspective, change needs to happen in the dominant culture. Few therapeutic strategies focus on loosening the rigid or dominant social constructions that constrain, influence, and oppress the life options of clients, as individuals, families, and members of ethnic groups.

Coconstructivist Perspectives

Coconstructive theories (Becvar & Becvar, 1994; Ivey, 2000; Neimeyer & Neimeyer, 1994) draw from both constructivist and social constructionist perspectives, and the intrapersonal and interpersonal domains. These models acknowledge the "need to shift back and forth between environmental and organismic reference points, assigning top priority to neither" (Prawat & Floden, 1994, p. 45). How we define self, self-in-relation, and context is coconstructed in constant person-environment transactions (Ivey et al., 2002) involving individuals, relationships, and the social realities that emerge from these transactions. Thus coconstructive models recognize a need to balance attention to internalized cognition and emotion with equal attention to how the client influences and is influenced by the wider social contexts of family, community, and culture (Rigazio-DiGilio et al., 1997). Clinicians form partnerships with clients designed to promote change in inner thoughts and feelings and in how they participate in their wider sociopolitical contexts (Ivey, 2000; Ivey et al., 2002; Locke, 1992; Rigazio-DiGilio, 2000; Rigazio-DiGilio et al., 1997).

Berger and Luckmann (1966) describe social constructions as the consensual recognition of the realness and rightness of a constructed reality, plus the socialization process by which people acquire this reality. Thus culture and language assume greater prominence during treatment, in the definition and resolution of the presenting problems. Coconstructivists pay particular attention to how language is used to define and influence the power differentials that infuse the interactions between individuals and their environments. Such a view of language-in-use leads inevitably to an analysis of power relations, whether at the level of individuals (e.g., within a marriage), groups (e.g., professional societies), or cultures (e.g., competing nations). Seen in this frame, power is not so much the property of persons, groups, or institutions, as it is a process of constructing a discourse that legitimates some form of social control over others, or even over oneself (Neimeyer, 1998).

The focus of coconstructivist therapies, then, is to surface the client's worldviews that are shared with significant others and to examine the power arrangements embedded in the languaging systems that govern the roles and identities the client has assumed. Helping clients recognize how to alter and modify the linguistic, power, and social contextual variables contributing to their meaning-making processes become the focus of coconstructivist counseling, and the community genogram is one tool to help clients describe these variables.

COCONSTRUCTIVIST TREATMENT

The goal of coconstructivist counseling is to use the client's language to sustain a therapeutic conversation until the coconstructed narrative that emerges no longer contains that which was experienced as a problem (Monk, 1997). One way to accomplish this is to explore various aspects of how clients understand and interpret their issues. Formulation of a treatment goal that fits with the client's idiosyncratic frame of reference is perhaps most important. It is crucial to learn how the client makes sense of the problem and to use this understanding as a point of departure to identify a workable goal for counseling (Guterman, 1994). The community genogram can be used to help clients share relevant information about critical times in their lives that can then be used to deconstruct rigid and constrictive narratives and to reconstruct viable new narratives that are liberating (Ivey, 2000) and empowering (Lyddon, 1995). The therapeutic goal, then, is to help the client win freedom from the dominant problem narratives and achieve genuine authorship of his or her life (Neimeyer & Raskin, 2000). The community genogram can be used in family work to identify potentially viable alternative stories and interpretations rather than attempting to identify particular characteristics of a presumed underlying psychopathology.

The Therapeutic Stance

In a coconstructivist approach to systemic work, counseling is viewed as a conversational context or dialogical space (Goolishian & Anderson, 1987) where counselors assume a collaborative role and become an equal, not superior, member of the therapeutic alliance. The therapeutic conversation generated within this alliance is a mutual search and exploration through an interactive exchange in which new meanings are continually evolving toward the "dis-solving" of problems. To accomplish a sense of mutuality, the therapist assumes the position of nonexpert or what Anderson and Goolishian refer to as a "not-knowing" stance. This "entails a general attitude or stance in which the therapist's actions communicate an abundant, genuine curiosity" (Anderson & Goolishian, 1992, p. 29). To "not-know" is not to have an unfounded or inexperienced judgment, but refers to a set of assumptions the counselor brings to the interview, such as the importance of learning the client's worldview, taking the client's story seriously, and knowing how to interpret the client's journey toward new self-identity. The community genogram facilitates client narratives about his or her individual and system life stories in a context where members of the therapeutic alliance can be listeners and mutual explorers. From these stories, multiple perspectives and interpretations can be generated to help reconstruct individual and system narratives that can support positive growth and development. The community genogram provides one vehicle where all members of the couple, family, or network can share their stories in order to create new understandings and resources.

The Role of Contextual and Developmental Variables

Unlike some family therapy approaches, such as strategic and structural, coconstructivists pay careful attention to the client's developmental and contextual histories. The stories and narratives that clients bring to treatment have been honed over their life span within a unique environmental context. The cultures within which they developed have influenced those stories and narratives, as have the particular communities, social groups, and familial contexts through which they have journeyed to create their current sense of self-in-relation. To coconstructivists, the relationship between development and context is intertwined: Clients' systems development is a function of their context and their context is a function of their system constructions. The community genogram brings out the latent and hidden dimensions of this interactive process and helps clients view how their developmental journeys influenced and were influenced by the contexts in which they grew up.

If the goal of coconstructivist methods is to empower clients to create viable new identities that account for contextual and cultural variables, then counseling must seek to realign power differentials that in the past served to marginalize the client. Coconstructivism therefore challenges therapists to move beyond a predominant focus on clients' interpersonal mental phenomena and become more knowledgeable of social, political, and economic barriers that impede personal development—barriers that profoundly affect persons who are members of marginalized groups (Efran & Cook, 2000). When contextual and cultural factors are directly addressed in the mutuality of coconstructivist counseling, the potential to enhance our clients' sociopolitical awareness as well as serving as a precursor to client social involvement and action increases (Lyddon, 1995). The community genogram is a tool specifically designed to focus the therapeutic dialogue on the contextual and developmental factors deemed important by clients.

Coconstructing Culturally Responsive Treatment Plans

Coconstructivist treatment plans attempt to account for the idiosyncratic ways that clients make meaning of their experience, including the influences of ethnic heritage, gender, class, age, and power. In this fashion, these methods are compatible with treatment methods that incorporate multicultural and feminist perspectives because all narratives are viewed as embedded stories within a community and cultural context. The community genogram can be used to redress cultural forces that have oppressed the client in the past and identify new cultural and community resources that can empower new self-identities of the client.

Coconstructivist interventions are designed to help clients examine the discrepancies that arise between their tightly held constructs and alternative ways of construing the same experience. The community genogram can be used to help clients look at the same experience from several different points of view. For example, any other person mentioned in the client's genogram can be "activated" by asking the client to present how that person would perceive the same event. In family therapy, different perspectives are immediately available in the counseling setting as other members can be asked to comment on the information contained in the community genogram.

A vast array of dialectic and dialogic questioning techniques are available to the coconstructivist therapist using narrative methods. The questions used in the following case study are intended to illustrate the kind of questions counselors can use to facilitate the construction and analysis of a community genogram. General descriptions of questioning strategies designed to explore meanings (Freedman & Combs, 1996), generate client self-descriptions (Durrant & Kowalski, 1993), explore exceptions to the rule (De Shazer, 1991), surface subjugated knowledges (White & Epston, 1990), stimulate personal and collective reflections (Adams-Westcott, Dafforn, & Sterne, 1993), focus positive asset searches (Ivey et al., 2002), and magnify the amplification of change and competence (O'Hanlon & Weiner-Davis, 1989) can be found throughout our professional literature. Worden (2003) summarizes Tomm's (1988) articulation of linear, circular, strategic, and reflexive questions that may be used in all counseling environments. Community genograms can be used with any systemic treatment method to help sustain awareness of community-related issues throughout the counseling process.

Change or transformation in our situated constructions occurs through a re-storying process based on differentiation and integration (McLeod, 1997). Through the process of differentiation, clients are assisted to generate rival narratives that are essentially equally plausible stories about the same event. Here multiple representations are elicited, which provide new explanations and possibilities. During the integration process clients construct a new, even more compelling story that can help them break free from the abstractions that can come to dominate the way they perceive the world (Efran & Cook, 2000). These narrative methods introduce incongruity and conflict inherent in clients' multiple representations and the goal of re-storying is to empower clients to construct healing and normalizing personal theories of what happened, why it happened, and what can be done about it (Gonçalves, 1995; Martin, 1988; Meichenbaum, 1994). The community genogram can assist in the differentiation and integration processes by helping clients examine various interpretations of significant events in their life's journey.

Guiding Client Progress Toward Termination

Coconstructivist treatment aims to conclude therapy with clients having a sense of optimism necessary for them to continue as their own therapists (Arciero & Guidano, 2000). During the termination phase of treatment, families can build on their new, broader narratives to negotiate with others more fluid identities that better utilize the resources of their communities and cultures (Neimeyer & Raskin, 2000). As with all models of treatment, termination begins long before the final session. As the last session approaches, coconstructivist therapists work with clients to cogenerate scaffolds to maintain and expand the more powerful and productive narratives they have developed during treatment.

By reviewing how meaning making might occur within families and therapy, you can link these theoretical conceptualizations to practice. The therapeutic relationship—like families—recycles through phases of development that are represented by different ways of making sense of and operating in the world or in therapy. Families make sense of their identity as collective systems and as systems-in-context, both over the life span and throughout the therapeutic process. These phases can be identified as *system exploration, consolidation, enhancement*, and *transformation* (Rigazio-DiGilio, 2000).

Individuals rely on their developmental and contextual histories to give meaning to and operate within relational contexts. In addition, these contexts elicit or constrain certain ways they come to understand themselves and others. In system exploration, individuals disclose perceptions and ideas about themselves and others as these evolve within the relational or therapeutic context. These interactions provide the stage upon which worldviews are tested, reinforced, and modified. It is the dialectic and recursive nature of these transactions that is the dynamic force of systems development. Over time a common ground is formed that provides a means to organize and make sense of continued exchanges (system consolidation). As exchanges expand to include a multitude of therapeutic or life span tasks, individuals and systems reflect on and extend their ways of making sense of and participating with one another and the wider surround (system enhancement). As these interactions continue, personal and therapeutic relationships will experience further internal and external pressures to change, which can be supportive, disconfirming, or oppressive. As these relationships adapt to and/or influence these forces of change, they move beyond outdated worldviews and reconstruct alternative perspectives and options that provide continuity for the relationship and influence necessary changes among individuals, relationships, and wider contexts (system transformation).

Judiciously interspersing opportunities for families to use different lenses on their developmental history allows for the sharing of perceptions in a concrete fashion. The ability to entertain multiple perspectives from a developmental framework, to isolate and maximize assets and strengths, to negotiate and secure resources in their community contexts, and to modify their narratives and behaviors in response to ever-changing circumstances in therapy and over the life span are useful milestones in therapy and can continue to be part of their guidance system after treatment has ended. A community genogram used once or multiple times throughout treatment can facilitate the development of these important skills. The original community genogram constructed by the family, as well as any subsequent genograms, can be a powerful reminder of the progress the family has made and provides a concrete scaffold from which to develop enduring positive narratives. A final community genogram not only portrays the relational and cultural supports that will be necessary to sustain the therapeutic gains beyond treatment but also brings closure to their work.

The case material in the next section illustrates how to create and maintain a therapeutic relationship within a coconstructivist perspective. To demonstrate the various ways community genogram questioning strategies and diagrammatic accountings can be incorporated across phases of treatment, we compressed real-life circumstances provided by a nonclinical couple in a series of interviews exploring their individual, couple, and family development-in-context. What follows is a portrait of coconstructivist treatment that uses this data, including excerpts from the interviews, to highlight some of the ways the community genogram can be utilized in couple and family counseling and therapy.

A PORTRAIT OF TREATMENT: THE CASE OF TINA AND KATHY

Kathy (44) and Tina (38) are partners living in Michigan. They met in June 1996, told each other that they really cared for one another July 10, and moved in together in their first apartment in Louisiana within a year. As a couple, they relocated from Louisiana about 3 years ago and are now planning to assume custody of Kathy's two children. Anna (15) is Kathy's biological daughter and plans on attending the local high school. Kristi (13) was adopted by Kathy and her then-husband Jim at age one. Kathy and Tina are preparing for the transition of the children from Jim, still living in Louisiana, to Kathy. In this simulated case, the community genogram is used at several junctures in treatment to highlight prior personal and collective narratives and to solidify a plan of action to reintegrate the children into Kathy and Tina's home.

Background Information

Settling in Michigan brought a new job for Kathy at a large university, a new comfortable home where the couple could be together without feeling guilty and ashamed, and various employment transitions for Tina. It was tremendously difficult for them. Kathy had to come without her children and Tina had the impression that "this isn't going to be OK."

At first the move was very isolating and there was a lack of community support. Kathy even called to get a job back in Louisiana. On the other hand, their new community would allow her and Tina to live in a more open fashion and Kathy did have a job where she could be open.

Tina also was struggling to find a job. Not working was very difficult because Tina had been a minister in a prestigious church in Louisiana. In Michigan she would have to start a new career path outside the ministry. After 6 months, she secured a receptionist position within a large corporation and began to move up quickly. At the time of treatment, the move had devastated the couple financially, which placed stress on their relationship and caused conflicts between them.

In response to the question, "How did you meet?" Tina explained, "I was Kathy's minister at the time." Kathy explained, "I had known Tina, as a person, for a long time and never previously experienced any attraction to her." Tina was attracted to Kathy immediately but was afraid to say anything. Tina thought Kathy was beautiful, smart, funny, and had a whole lot of energy, and she really liked her. These were attributes she was seeking in her own life.

Kathy and Tina's relationship developed gradually over regular lunches to talk about church-related issues. At first Tina was so quiet that Kathy wondered about her. Tina noted, "I was afraid to say anything to mess up the relationship." A turning point occurred in their relationship when Tina found a lump in her breast. Kathy brought Tina a six-pack of coke. Kathy hugged Tina and made a gesture—touching her hair—to express her interest to Tina.

They were now preparing for a change that could be more drastic than the move north. A relational community genogram was used to surface the personal narratives that each member brought into the relationship. They were asked to identify the significant others (placed in channels) and the major life events (depicted as embayments) happening in their lives at the time of their coming together. Figure 6.1 reflects the essential contextual and developmental factors that influenced their joining. They were asked to include information about their families-of-procreation and families-of-origin.

Exploring Contextual and Transgenerational Forces

As two individuals come together to form a family, each brings life scripts emanating from their own families-of-origin. The community genogram can be used to focus on influences stemming from transgenerational factors. Kathy and Tina were asked to comment on the factors represented in their relational community genogram.

Therapist: What was happening previously in your family-of-origin and family-of-procreation to influence joining?

Kathy's family-of-procreation. Kathy discussed elements of her community genogram (see Figure 6.1). "I was working at a major university and had two children, but I was in an unhappy marriage with little physical intimacy. My husband was a good parent to our two children and a good physician—but the marriage was not going well. It was during this time that I had the sense that I was gay and was interested in and attracted to women."

Kathy's family-of-origin. "My mother's death when I was in college was very significant. Since that time I had a decreased connection with my family-of-origin. Although I tried to reconnect after having children, it turns out that a stronger connection was made with my husband's family-of-origin."

Tina's family-of-procreation. As indicated in Figure 6.1, Tina indicated that she had been divorced four years earlier from a marriage that also was unfulfilling and seemed wrong. "I knew that I had been avoiding going home and dove into my work to avoid being home with my husband. I had known I was gay since I was a child. I had my first relationship with a woman when I was in college. I thought that somehow I would make myself become heterosexual."

Tina's family-of-origin. "Prior to my divorce there was little distinction between my family-of-procreation and my family-of-origin. My mother had been very involved in my marital relationship. My ultimate divorce was very difficult for mom and this caused a disconnection with my family-of-origin. It was at this time I met Kathy, and my mother just had been diagnosed with breast cancer."

FIGURE 6.1. Kathy and Tina's Relational Community Genogram: Joining of the Couple

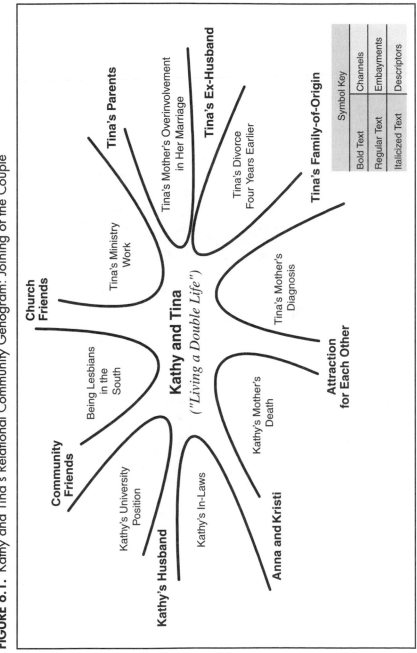

Community Friends

Kathy's Husband

Church Friends

Tina's Parents

Tina's Ex-Husband

Kathy's University Position

Being Lesbians in the South

Tina's Ministry Work

Tina's Mother's Overinvolvement in Her Marriage

Tina's Divorce Four Years Earlier

Kathy's In-Laws

Kathy and Tina
(*"Living a Double Life"*)

Kathy's Mother's Death

Tina's Mother's Diagnosis

Tina's Family-of-Origin

Anna and Kristi

Attraction for Each Other

Symbol Key	
Bold Text	Channels
Regular Text	Embayments
Italicized Text	Descriptors

The Wider Context

Therapist: As you two started living together, what was happening with work, friends, community, and wider contexts to influence your joining?

Tina summed up the time this way: "It was very difficult. We were two women who were leaving our husbands and were 'conveniently living together.' People in the community really had suspicions, but what could they say? But it was a small town, and the message we got from the community was negative."

Kathy noted, "People from the church came up to Tina asking her if she was with me, and she would say that we were just friends. And they said, 'If you are with her then that means you're a lesbian.' Because of the lack of acceptance from others we were leading a 'double' life. If Tina's church had found out, she would have been kicked out, publicly humiliated, and brought up on charges! This situation made Tina feel very anxious and often physically ill. I, on the other hand, was afraid of getting in legal trouble, losing my children and being poor."

At that time, Kathy and Tina, through therapy, realized that they were very committed to their relationship despite all the difficulties it would cause. Eventually, they decided that Tina needed to quit her position at church. Interestingly enough, Tina got well immediately upon the presentation of her resignation papers.

After deciding that she really wanted to be with Tina, Kathy didn't feel it was right to stay in her relationship with husband Jim. Kathy explained, "Jim suggested we go to counseling, but I told the therapist that I was going to leave. Jim eventually began to suspect about my secret life. He used threats to get me to stay. He told me I would have to leave the house with nothing and no kids. It was critical that Tina and I had to keep the lie going so Jim couldn't use this against me."

Kathy and Jim divorced. It took a year for the divorce to become final. Kathy didn't ask for anything, and she retained joint custody of the children. Kathy's children stayed with her while Jim worked (he worked 15 days on, 15 days off). Kathy reports, "The kids had fun when they stayed over and we did lots of things together." Kathy told Anna about Tina and Kathy's relationship the day the divorce was final. Anna didn't have any problems with the relationship and understood why they didn't tell her about the relationship earlier.

Tina's memory of that time frame centered on her relationship with her mother. "My mother had supported me all her life, and I, in my own way, supported her. So naturally I thought the support would just continue. I knew it would be difficult for mom to accept my relationship with Kathy, but I felt she would adjust to it. I always assumed she would still love me. But when I told mom, she just cried and cried. She fell apart and was miserable. She told me that I had ruined her life."

Therapist: What was happening in your work, friends, community, and wider contexts to influence staying together in Louisiana?

Tina and Kathy said that lesbian couples approached them and told them that they had to keep their relationship secret. As Tina recalls, "One member of a lesbian couple who was a very powerful figure in the community—she was a lawyer and also chair of the finance committee at church—warned us about the importance of keeping our relationship secret. This woman and her partner maintained the pretext of being in a heterosexual relationship by still being married and living with their husbands and their children. We received many similar messages that made us feel that we had to keep our relationship secret. After a while, gay men and women approached us and revealed that they were gay. Eventually we had a friendship circle of three lesbian couples and we all had to keep this quiet. We felt like we were part of the underground. In Louisiana, we never knew one 'out' person. We never noticed rainbows on cars."

In terms of finances, together they had not much experience working with budgets. Neither had been well prepared to manage finances in their relationship. Kathy puts it this way: "We didn't have much money. I had to learn new spending habits and this wasn't easy, but compared to Tina it was nothing, as she lost her whole career."

Therapist: As you reflect on these aspects of your mutual community genogram so far, what are your thoughts and reflections?

Kathy stated, "Looking back, it seems that we did some things that didn't really show good judgment. It's almost like we were volcanoes that had suppressed so much for so long that was part of it—we found this meeting of each other (mine was a crummy marriage—no sex) and then this being a lesbian thing—I was doubly suppressed. Obviously, there is some shame about some of the things we did to other people, like our husbands and family members—it wasn't kind. We weren't the type of people to say, 'Oh, we'll wait until we are completely out of our [former] relationships—which we heard other people do—and then we will be together.' We didn't do that."

Tina noted, "We knew people who had waited a year or more to get together. They never did anything physical until they got out of the other relationship." Kathy added, "We also knew women who spent 20 years still married. At least we didn't do that. I guess the decisions you make have to do with what you can live with." Kathy summed it up when she said, "We were doing the best we could."

Therapist: What are the major themes you detect from this exploration?

Tina answered, "I think that two things stand out for me. First, we followed our hearts, and regardless of the amount of negativity we had to deal with, we stayed together. Second, it's sad to realize that our families and friends were not able to accept our relationship and they really made it difficult. This analysis tells me how important family and friends are." She stated emphatically, "When the kids come, it will be important to have a wide network of friends to help ease the transition."

Kathy concurred: "I think our judgment is much better today and we no longer have to deal with others accepting our relationship. I think we'll be able to help the kids and it's important to keep the lines of communication open and really listen, even if they tell us things we may not want to hear."

In sum, the initial analysis of the community genogram raises many relational, developmental, familial, and contextual forces that have shaped Tina's and Kathy's history. The community genogram brought these issues to the surface in a concrete fashion so that they could tell their individual sides of their mutual history.

Coconstructing a Culturally Responsive Plan for Tina and Kathy

Based on Tina's and Kathy's wish to explore issues of helping Kathy's adolescent children adjust to their new home, the counselor invited Kathy and Tina to each do an individual community genogram when they were teenagers to identify intergenerational themes.

The Teenage Years: Tina

We use Tina's community genogram presented in Figure 6.2 as a background to the narrative information. We begin this analysis with the therapist's question focusing on this examination.

Therapist: Tina, what are you aware of as you examine your community genogram?

Self. "What's most notable for me is the lack of self. The embayments and channels push in to the center leaving me precious little space for self.

FIGURE 6.2. Tina's Adolescent Community Genogram

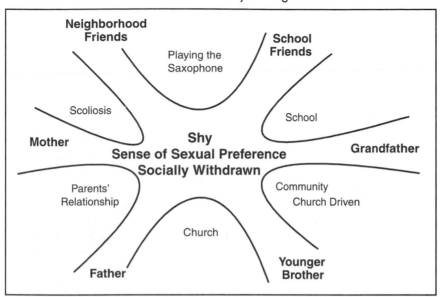

As a teenager, I was socially withdrawn. I was significantly involved with playing the alto sax. I had a sense that I was gay, but this was not acceptable in my house."

Tina's Significant Others

Mother. Tina notes that "the large channel represents the significant influence my mother had on me at the time." Her mother was very intellectual but also went through alternating phases of high energy and low energy. Tina states, "Mom's always been overly involved with me—I was going to be everything she wasn't and I played that role for years. . . . I was the only one who could make her happy even during her depressions." Tina had been aware of this pattern of behaviors since the age of 8. "It was difficult, I couldn't live up to it, mixed with some specialness. I found it impossible to maintain."

During adolescence Tina's mother is a dominant influence. "Mom's messages are strong. Because of my severe case of scoliosis I had to wear a back brace and my mother wanted me to survive adolescence. She knew this would be a difficult time with the back brace." During this time her mother had an affair with a preacher—and thereafter Tina had a deep distrust of her parents and experienced the instability it caused at home.

Father. The smaller channel in the genogram represents less influence. "He's more fun than mom. I see him as a 'weak' male, who worked in the same place all his life and hated his job. His advice to me was, 'Get your job, keep your job, do your job, love your family, take care of your family.'" Tina enjoyed fishing with him and has many positive memories of this.

Brother. The big channel reveals a strong influence—"larger than my father's. My parents described my younger brother as a 'gift to Tina.' I was involved in naming him." Tina was very close to him and described their relationship as "strong and positive."

Grandfather (paternal). Tina spent a lot of time with him. "He let me do whatever I wanted to do." She loved working with him—getting dirty, working with tools, driving tractors. He never got mad at her and "I experienced acceptance and freedom . . . he was a very positive influence."

School friends. Tina reported that she had very few close friends during high school due to her medical issues.

Neighborhood friends. Tina had little contact with them. Some friends would come over for Sunday school that was held at their house but it was a rare occurrence.

Embayments in Tina's Community Genogram

Parents' relationship. "They fought a lot. My mother was dominant in the relationship. They didn't seem to share much. Mom regularly threatened to leave—this was a big influence on me. Even if they stick with it, they might be lying to you." Her mother's affair with the preacher was always present in Tina's mind.

Church. Church was a large influence on Tina. Besides her mother's affair with the preacher, Tina was aware of significant messages from church, such as, "you couldn't be angry, give your life to God, there are 'right ways' to do things." Tina was aware that these rules applied differently to different people.

Community. Her community was a rural southern town with many churches and one store. "The town was church driven. Certain families went to certain churches. Some churches had more status. My church was huge; it had a very strong influence in the community."

School. Tina didn't go to school for a year due to the surgery and recovery. To Tina, "doing school work at home was great." The tutor who came to help her was very nice.

Music. Music was one outlet Tina had at this time. She played alto sax in a band.

Scoliosis. In 7th grade Tina had to get a back brace. "I had to wear it all day with the exception of 2 hours. Nobody else at school had one, and I just shut down and stayed at home. My adolescence was a time of major withdrawal. I did play in a band but that was the extent of my leaving the house. I wore the brace for 2 years, and then in 8th grade I found out I had to have surgery. Mom took it hard. Following the surgery, I had to wear a cast and continued with the brace through 12th grade. Other children left me alone, so I kept to myself. I couldn't be angry because I was a 'Christian.' I had very few dates during this time."

Therapist: Tina, as you now have looked at this community genogram, what thoughts are you aware of?

Tina responded, "I see foundations of my low sense of self. This was a difficult period for me. From having to wear the brace and being withdrawn to begin with, I learned to be alone. During this time mom also pulled back, she was less intrusive because of the back brace. So I was unhappy and miserable. I couldn't wait to get out of high school.

"Oh, I dated boys because that's what I was supposed to do—even though I knew I was gay. I was following messages from my mom—go out on dates; you're supposed to like boys. I knew there were women in church who were gay. In private, my mom would tell me how bad it was. I really thought that I would change if I just acted a different way. I would say to myself, I'm gonna have to figure out a way to think differently. I can train myself to like men. I thought that if I did something long enough I would change."

Now let's turn to Kathy's community genogram presented in Figure 6.3. Kathy's narrative illustrates her perceptions of key influences when she was an adolescent.

Self. Kathy's sense of self as an adolescent is reflected by her placement in the center of the community genogram. "My identity is very connected with play and sports. During high school I was compliant; I didn't drink, smoke, or have sex. I didn't break rules until college. I attended a liberal Baptist college and the ideas expressed there helped me move away from my parents' ideas." She also moved away from a belief in the literal interpretation of the Bible. These transitions all occurred while her mother was dying.

Kathy's Significant Others

Mother and father. Kathy's community genogram depicts a very clear boundary between children and parents. Kathy says, "Sometimes the parental hierarchy was shifted by my older brother's power. My mother was quite busy with family, friends, and church. When she stood up for others, she would be very strong. I felt she was the heart of my family. She decided what the

FIGURE 6.3. Kathy's Adolescent Community Genogram

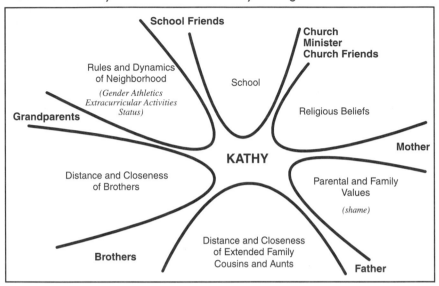

family would do: the travel, weekend trips, etc. Father was no fun. He spent a great deal of time at work. He followed and enforced the rules in a concrete and inflexible fashion."

Kathy's discussion of her adolescence focused on the illusion that her mother was very involved in her life. Kathy felt that she had little access to her mother. Her mother had cancer when Kathy was in high school and died 5 years later when Kathy was in college. Her mother had high expectations of Kathy. She wanted Kathy to marry someone like Billy Graham and do something related to religion.

Kathy notes, "It was very important for me to be spiritual, from my mother's point of view. I never questioned my parents' rules. The only time a discussion like that occurred was when my mother was dying. It was only between her and me, but she hinted that if we had had more time, she might be persuaded to accept my different ways of looking at life."

Kathy described her parents' marriage as "not really good." Her mother did express some of her unhappiness. Her advice to Kathy was to "marry someone who really shows their love for you." Her mother grew up in an alcoholic and chaotic family. Kathy sensed that her mother got security and stability from her husband. He was rigid. He came from a rigid and concrete family. As a couple, Kathy describes them "as a typical couple—they hated each other. They hated the things that they married each other for."

Siblings. Kathy has two brothers, Paul and Rodney. Rodney was a very powerful older brother. Paul was close in age to Kathy and they played a lot together. Kathy notes that the sibling relationships interconnected with her friends and neighborhood relationships. During adolescence Kathy noted there was some conflict with her brothers, but for the most part they all got along.

Cousins. Of the extended family Kathy notes that there was one cousin with whom she went to church and school. In high school, she hung with a different crowd. For the most part, her cousins were peripheral in her life, but still in the picture, particularly at family gatherings.

Church friends. These friends were different than the friends Kathy played with at home. Kathy played with them on weekends when her family went away with their church friends.

School friends. These friends were separate from the ones at church. Very few school friends were neighborhood friends and there was not a strong connection with any of these friends. After high school Kathy did not keep in touch with these friends.

Grandparents. Kathy notes that neither set of grandparents played an active role in her life during her teenage years. "They were not really involved. My father's parents were cold and disinterested. My mother's parents lived far away and were poor. We perceived ourselves as better off than my maternal grandparents. This perception was clearly what my father believed. Even my mother was condescending to them."

Embayments in Kathy's Community Genogram

Religious values/doctrines. Kathy's family was very involved with the church. Kathy attributes her strong sense of guilt to her Baptist background. "It gave me a very clear sense of right and wrong. When I could get to college and had to think for myself, I really appreciated the foundation gained from the church. It gave me a strong sense of self and deep confidence in my belief system. I learned the Bible very well, and now I use this as a resource from which to argue with people." Her experience with the church gave her the sense of "You should stand for something" and it's appropriate to "put yourself out for others." According to Kathy, the religious pressures combined with the parental influence to send strong messages about control and guilt. There was no notion about forgiveness or grace, no room for error or mistakes. "You could always be better."

Parental influence and family beliefs. Kathy reported that her parents communicated a strong message. "You had to be tough, even when you got hurt. So what, you are still alive!" This belief pushed her to be really good at things. On the other hand, it led to a decrease in empathy for others. Her family did not express feelings openly, nor share interests freely. In her family, you were ridiculed for your mistakes. "You were expected to act like things were always under control. There was no room to question or challenge family rules."

Kathy also recalled how her family was very insular. Her family acted as if they were better than others. Often they criticized others—even friends. However, Kathy would forgive friends and show tolerance toward others. This set up differences with her family. She cites her father and older brother's influence on the family, and although her mother was soft and kind, she was not strong enough. The message from the family was, "if you are not criticizing, others will be doing it."

Extended family. The extended family was minimal at this time.

Siblings. Kathy's older brother, Rodney had a great deal of power in the family. When he broke rules, Kathy's parents threatened him and punished him at first, but nothing changed. Her parents just stopped finding out what he was doing. They instituted a "don't ask, don't tell" policy. "He had a lot of control on the family because he went to a local college until his junior year."

Social environment. Although Kathy had friends at church and in her neighborhood, she didn't have close friendships. Her social interactions were largely around sports and she was involved with siblings and a small group of neighborhood and school friends.

School environment. Kathy was popular in school. She hung around with the "in" crowd and was active in tennis and other sports. This was very important to Kathy. What was notable about this period was that in school she remembers being very attracted to all her female teachers. She wanted to be with them, to hang around them. Kathy knew there was something going on with her that was weird.

Therapist: Kathy, as you share these images, what stands out from this process?

"I really had very definite beliefs about what was right and what was wrong. I held on very strongly to those ideas. Now I can see that I was making simplistic distinctions and that there's much more gray in the world. It's not as easy as 'that's wrong all the time' or 'that's the only way to think.' When I was an adolescent, I was a Christian, and I did not hide it. Now, I'm gay, and I am going to be gay, and I am not going to hide that.

"Strengths at this time were that I learned how to have fun and to be competitive. I learned how to look like I had confidence in myself—like I knew what I was doing. My family also taught me not to follow what people tell you, really reinforcing my autonomy.

"Sexually, I had a sense from childhood that I was attracted to women. But I certainly didn't think about it, nor would I talk about it. I do wonder if I married someone, a man, who was sexually open, then maybe I wouldn't have to be with a woman exclusively. However, after being with a woman, I just knew I was gay. On the other hand, if it had been a more accepting society—where a person could just be attracted to another and you could talk about your attractions as a child—I would have known that I was gay at a much earlier age."

Therapist: What individual or collective themes are evident in these genograms to the both of you?

Kathy and Tina noted that there were significant similarities operating during their adolescence. Kathy stated, "We both were strongly connected to our church, neither one of us had a strong peer network, and we both had difficulty being with our parents." They both agreed that their home would have to be very different if they wanted Kathy's children to be happy.

This issue became the focus during the middle part of the treatment. The contextualized analysis of their adolescence helped Kathy and Tina gain a new perspective about the choices and resources they now have in their lives to create a different, more supportive atmosphere for the two teenage girls entering their home.

Tina and Kathy's Final Joint Community Genogram

Wanting to use the self-knowledge that was generated by the analysis of the two prior community genograms, the therapist asked Tina and Kathy to construct another joint diagram about how they would like to see the future unfold so that they could fully support Kathy's children. Tina and Kathy's final relational community genogram was viewed as a blueprint for the couple to follow to make the transition a positive one. The last three sessions of treatment concentrated on helping Tina and Kathy create the situations depicted in Figure 6.4.

Family Constellation. Tina and Kathy placed Anna and Kristi in the middle of the community genogram. Kathy explains, "We have to help them feel welcomed. Tina and I felt this would not be too difficult. I have maintained a very positive relationship with the children when we were in Louisiana and the children expressed a great desire to join us in Michigan." Tina noted that this would be difficult to achieve immediately. "The children will have to adjust to me and to our relationship. I think there's going to be some competition as to who gets more quality time with Kathy." Kathy agreed that planning for this would be important.

FIGURE 6.4. Tina and Kathy's Relational Community Genogram: The Future

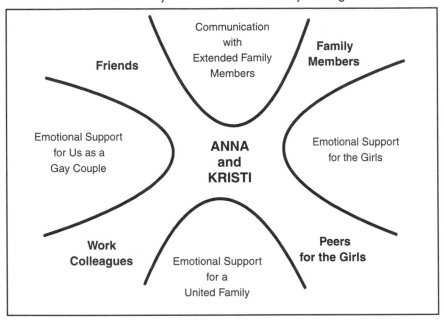

Friends. Kathy and Tina are still not totally sure how the community will respond to them as a gay couple—particularly with children coming into their lives. They plan to take their rainbow stickers off their cars temporarily. For them, this will be a major concession. The stickers are their way of connecting with others who are gay. There is a sense for Kathy that they are taking a major step backward in their openness. For Tina, this is a gap or like taking a little break. They will take the stickers off for a while. They will see if it is OK and then determine if they need to put the stickers back.

Work colleagues. Both Kathy and Tina state that their friends at work will be very supportive. Kathy has recently left the university to start her own business, and she is certain that her colleagues are aware and supportive of Kathy reuniting with her children. Tina's work colleagues are very supportive, but they probably won't be adding any substantive help because they don't visit outside the office now.

Peers for the girls. Kathy expressed the concern both women felt. "Since we realized we won't be able to choose their friends for them, we know that we must do whatever it takes to help them adjust to a new school. We have contacted the local YWCA to find out about drama clubs for Anna and horseback riding for Kristi—activities they each like. Again, this is going to be an ongoing area of concern."

Family members. There are no family relatives in the immediate area. All of the extended family is in the South so there should not be any conflicts that interfere with the children's integration at this time.

Embayments

Emotional support for the couple. Kathy and Tina feel stronger together as a couple. Tina's language captures the feelings, "we expect there will be more difficulties to come and more challenges, but we feel confident we can face them together. Certainly, we are more financially secure and have established strong career paths. Emotionally we have never been happier. We worked through the relocation and have succeeded in solving problems that could stress other couples to the point of breakup. We feel we have emerged from this experience as a stronger, more loving couple."

Emotional support for the girls. Together Kathy and Tina discussed ways to create open lines of communication for each of the girls. They know that each girl has separate needs and that they would have to allow for each one's individuality. As Kathy puts it, "because we are unable to control the peer and school interactions, we both think that this area of support is the most difficult to ensure. Issues of dating and how to help the girls develop a healthy sense of self as sexual beings will also be issues as they mature."

Emotional support for the united family. The size of this embayment denotes the importance of this area for Kathy and Tina. They recognize that the blended family will need a lot of patience, and that there will be much boundary testing. The exploration of this area generated numerous questions. "Will the girls compete against each other and Tina for Kathy's attention and affection? How will the girls receive Tina's parental authority? How will Kathy and Tina support the launching of Anna and how will it affect Kristi? How will both girls react to community messages about gay families?"

Communication with members of the extended family. Questions about how to help Anna and Kristi feel accepted by other members of Kathy's and Tina's family filled this embayment. "How will the extended families react to the girls living with Kathy and Tina? Although Jim accepts this arrangement now," Kathy noted, "others—such as Tina's father and my brothers may not be as accepting. We realize work is needed in this area also, but it will come later. Fortunately, we don't plan on a lot of interaction with these relatives soon, but inevitably we know we will have to deal with them. For instance, when Anna graduates and other holidays and special events, we will have to consider how to communicate with our extended families."

The Outcome for Tina and Kathy

This community genogram helped Kathy and Tina anticipate some of the difficult areas that will have to be worked through to effectively reunite Kathy with her children. The community genogram was also used to consider resources inside and outside the couple that would help make this integration a positive experience. The remainder of counseling focused on these issues, and then the couple decided that within the first 3 months of the girls living with them they would all return for a few sessions to be sure that everyone's needs were being accepted and dealt with.

CONCLUSION: ILLUSTRATING THE STORY LINE

In this chapter the community genogram is shown as both an assessment tool and an intervention strategy, specifically within a coconstructivist framework. Its value as a communication device is evident in the multiple ways the community genogram can stimulate past, present, and future needs and contextual dynamics of family clients. While it is contextualized within a postmodern approach to counseling, the community genogram is a convivial tool that can complement any form of individual or systems treatment method.

Throughout this chapter the types of questions counselors can use have been illustrated. The intent and focal point of the question can lead clients to elaborate their narrative during treatment. These extensions may contain resources heretofore not perceived by our clients. Even memories that elicit unpleasant emotions can be used to inform decisions being made by clients to enhance their lives now and in the future. The flexibility of the community genogram permits clients to graphically represent their new narratives to solidify their plans for change.

Community genograms quickly raise issues that may not be surfaced in a verbal-only treatment format. The visual representations allow for multiple interpretations by the creator or any other member of the therapeutic alliance. If our goal is help clients feel more comfortable and connected to their immediate surround, then the community genogram is one easy and powerful device to help clients concretely see their sense of self-in-relation to others. Further, it helps identify the strengths and resources clients may overlook as they prepare for a new tomorrow.

Epilogue

There is no escape in psychotherapy from the requirement that the therapist become conscious of factors that might affect or condition the patient's reactions within the therapeutic situation or bear upon the patient's life outside that situation.
—J. Whol, "Psychotherapy and Cultural Diversity"

As the field of counseling and therapy continues to adapt to the technologically abundant and information-rich world, we search for methods of generating self-reflection and insight. Many methods, across multiple schools, are designed to generate personal and collective information to more fully appreciate the larger contextual influences that give meaning to the narrow personal story lines of our narratives. The community genogram is one more tool clinicians and educators can activate to promote self- and collective reflection.

USING THE COMMUNITY GENOGRAM WITHIN A LARGER REPERTOIRE OF CLINICAL PRACTICE

Clinicians are searching for more and more effective means to treatment. Even though the call for privileging evidence-based approaches to treatment is gaining prominence across the field, clinicians are still seeking the ability to select from among many possible therapeutic techniques that can be used with a particular client. The community genogram can be used to supplement any specific treatment approach and can be integrated across schools and models of counseling and therapy. The community genogram can be used to help inform the practitioner about which methods of treatment may be compatible with the client's background and style of learning.

The Community Genogram As an Assessment Tool

Helping clients adjust to a self-reflective environment can be very difficult and time-consuming. The community genogram can be used early in counseling to accelerate the formation of a therapeutic alliance and provide valuable information about the contextual factors that are influencing the client's worldview. Using the community genogram as an assessment tool, therapists can gain knowledge of the client's preferred thinking style, key historical and contextual factors, and the narrative methods toward which the client is predisposed. The open-ended usage of the community genogram provides a broad opening for clients to begin tracing the roots and evolution of issues that are currently impacting their lives. This historical focus sets the reflective process in motion and provides multiple entry points for the clinician. The actual elements of the community genogram, the method of telling the story, the impact of time and evolving relationships, as well as the current situation are all approachable through the graphic rendering. The concrete nature of the graphic representation and the conceptual synthesis required to connect past to present, facilitates a rapid assessment of issues which generated treatment for a wide spectrum of clientele. By using the community genogram at the initiation of service, a marker is established that can be used throughout the course of treatment to track progress and surface deeper, more latent issues embedded in the initial community genogram.

The Community Genogram As an Intervention device

The community genogram is a convivial tool that conforms to a variety of needs across the therapeutic journey. At key points in treatment the community genogram can be used to help clients focus deeply on particular issues. Unlike using the community genogram as an open-ended device, its intentional use in the middle of treatment can help reinforce or clarify essential forces operating on the clients' understanding of their current situation.

During the problem-identification process, the community genogram can help raise historical and contextual factors that might be overlooked or underappreciated in a more traditional verbal rendition of contributing factors. As treatment shifts toward the experimentation with solutions, the community genogram can be used to help identify previous positive episodes of change in the client's life. Similarly, during the termination phase of treatment, the community genogram can provide moral assistance for successful separation.

Beyond using the community genogram during specific stages of treatment, it can also be used to reinforce systemic and ecosystemic aspects of problem formation and solution generation. Helping clients realize that linear explanations of functioning are too narrow and are used to perpetuate cherished biases is essential for therapeutic change. The community genogram is an ideal tool to help clients see that reciprocal patterns of behavior influence functioning at the level of the individual, the dyad, the family or group, the community, and the culture. The community genogram can be used to help clients see the larger repeating and self-maintaining cycles of interaction over time and within specific contexts.

Finally, the community genogram is designed to help clients understand the socially constructed nature of problems and their effects. Often the societal forces and the interpersonal dynamics that shift the connotation of an idiosyncratic or natural response from positive to negative are difficult for clients to fully understand. The community genogram helps bring out these forces in clear relief and can be used in treatment to demonstrate the oppressive and controlling forces operating in the social realm. The community genogram helps focus on strengths within the client environment that can be used to alter the rigid definitions and connotations attached to particular behavior and thoughts. The power relationships operating in these environments can also be highlighted so that clients may make informed decisions about future actions.

The Community Genogram As an Evaluation Device

While the potential of the community genogram as a research tool was not addressed in this book, it is evident that the graphic representations can be quantitatively and qualitatively evaluated. The graphic reproduction and the accompanying narrative can be used to assess the client's level of contextual awareness. This awareness can be combined with other indicators of client progress to present a more comprehensive understanding of the change process. If understanding one's context and possessing the ability to influence, not merely to be influenced by, wider societal and community forces is associated with client success and satisfaction, then the community genogram is one method that could be considered to capture these factors. As all counseling and therapy moves closer to systemic and ecosystemic conceptualizations, we will need bridges to help clients and practitioners more fully appreciate the influence of past, present, and future contextual forces. The community genogram offers the field one such device.

CONCLUSION: THE IMPORTANCE OF CONTEXT

In the preceding chapters, a variety of formats for applying the techniques and methods of the community genogram have been presented. It is essential to realize that the concept of surfacing ecosystemic dynamics across time is the most important aim of this volume. The methods, such as the star diagram, the family floor plan, or community map, are merely means to an end. The creative practitioner will be able to infuse the use of spontaneous, as well as predetermined, visualizing opportunities in a seamless fashion to help clients identify and realize how contextual forces have influenced their lives. If you take one thing away from this book, it should be that *context matters*. We need to use a variety of strategies to raise complex issues in easily understandable formats.

While context matters, it is very often difficult to bring into the therapy or counseling setting. It can be overwhelming, emotionally and informationally. It is often difficult to get a wider view of context when we tightly hold onto cherished interpretations. It is often discussed, then discounted, and removed to the background, being superceded by preferred therapeutic methods. If your approach to therapy does not value and infuse context, it often will not be fully integrated into the treatment narrative. The community genogram is a simple technique that clients can quickly grasp and that we can continually refer to over the course of time.

References

Adams-Westcott, J., Dafforn, T. A., & Sterne, P. (1993). Escaping victim life stories and co-constructing personal agency. In S. Gilligan & R. Price (Eds.), *Therapeutic conversations* (pp. 258–276). New York: W. W. Norton.

Adler, A. (1926). *The neurotic constitution.* New York: Books for Libraries Press.

Anderson, H., & Goolishian, H. A. (1988). Human systems as linguistic systems: Preliminary and evolving ideas about the implications for clinical theory. *Family Process, 27,* 371–393.

Anderson, H., & Goolishian, H. A. (1992). The client is the expert. In S. McNamee & K. Gergen (Eds.), *Therapy as social construction* (pp. 67–79). Newbury Park, CA: Sage.

Angelou, M. (1970). *I know why the caged bird sings.* New York: Bantam.

Anthony, W., & Carkhuff, R. (1977). The functional professional therapeutic agent. In A. Gurman & A. Razin (Eds.), *Effective psychotherapy* (pp. 103–119). Elmsford, NY: Pergamon.

Arciero, G., & Guidano, V. F. (2000). Experience, explanation, and the quest for coherence. In R. A. Neimeyer & J. D. Raskin (Eds.), *Constructions of disorder* (pp. 91–118). Washington, DC: American Psychological Association.

Attneave, C. (1982). American Indian and Alaska native families: Emigrants in their own homeland. In M. McGoldrick, J. Pearce, & J. Giordano (Eds.), *Ethnicity and family therapy* (pp. 187–201). New York: Guilford Press.

Auerswald, E. (1983). The Gouveneur Health Service Program: An experiment in ecosystemic community care delivery. *Family Systems Medicine, 1,* 5–13.

Axelson, J. A. (1999). *Counseling and development in a multicultural society* (3rd ed.). Pacific Grove, CA: Brooks/Cole.

Banks, J. (2002). *An introduction to multicultural education* (3rd ed.). Boston: Allyn and Bacon.

Becvar, D. S., & Becvar, R. J. (2003). *Family therapy: A systemic integration* (5th ed.). Boston, MA: Allyn and Bacon.

Becvar, R. J., & Becvar, D. S. (1994). The ecosystemic story: A story about stories. *Journal of Mental Health Counseling, 16,* 22–32.

Berger, P., & Luckmann, T. (1966). *The social construction of reality.* Garden City, NY: Doubleday.

Bowen, M. (1978). *Family therapy in clinical practice.* New York: Jason Aronson.

Breunlin, D., Schwartz, R., & MacKune-Karrer, B. (1992). *Metaframeworks: Transcending the models of family therapy.* San Francisco: Jossey-Bass.

141

Bronfenbrenner, U. (1979). *The ecology of human development*. Cambridge, MA: Harvard University Press.

Brown, L. S. (2000). Discomforts of the powerless: Feminist constructions of distress. In R. A. Neimeyer & J. D. Raskin (Eds.), *Constructions of disorder* (pp. 287–308). Washington, DC: American Psychological Association.

Burr, V. (1995). *An introduction to social constructionism*. London: Routledge.

Cheatham, H. (1990). Empowering black families. In H. Cheatham & J. Stewart (Eds.), *Black families* (pp. 373–393). New Brunswick, NJ: Transaction Press.

Congress, E. P. (1994). The use of culturagrams to assess and empower culturally diverse families. *Families in Society: The Journal of Contemporary Human Services, 75*, 531–540.

Coopersmith, E. (1980). The family floor plan: A tool for training, assessment and intervention in family therapy. *Journal of Marital and Family Therapy, 6*, 141–145.

Cross, W. E., Jr. (1991). *Shades of black: Diversity in African American identity*. Philadelphia: Temple University Press.

D'Andrea, M. (2000). Postmodernism, constructivism, and multiculturalism: Three forces reshaping and expanding our thoughts about counseling. *Journal of Mental Health Counseling, 22*, 1–16.

D'Andrea, M., & Daniels, J. (2001). Respectful counseling: An integrative multidimensional model for counselors. In D. Pope-Davis & H. Coleman (Eds.), *The intersection of race, class, and gender in multicultural counseling* (pp. 417–466). Thousand Oaks, CA: Sage.

Daniels, M. H., & White, L. J. (1994). Human systems as problem-determined linguistic systems: Relevance for training, *Journal of Mental Health Counseling, 16*, 105–119.

Dell, P. (1982). Beyond homeostasis: Toward a concept of coherence. *Family Process, 21*, 21–24.

De Shazer, S. (1991). *Putting difference to work*. New York: W. W. Norton.

Duhl, F. J. (1981). The use of the chronological chart in general systems family therapy. *Journal of Marital and Family Therapy, 7*, 361–373.

Dunn, A. B., & Levitt, M. M. (2000). The genogram: From diagnostics to mutual collaboration. *Family Journal: Counseling and Therapy for Couples and Families, 8*, 236–244.

Durrant, M., & Kowalski, K. (1993). Enhancing views of competence. In S. Friedman (Ed.), *The new language of change: Constructive collaboration in psychotherapy* (pp. 107–137). New York: Guilford Press.

Efran, J. S., & Cook, P. E. (2000). Linguistic ambiguity as a diagnostic tool. In R. A. Neimeyer & J. D. Raskin (Eds.), *Constructions of disorder* (pp. 121–144). Washington, DC: American Psychological Association.

Falicov, C. J. (1988). Learning to think culturally. In H. A. Liddle, D. S. Breunlin, & R. C. Schwartz (Eds.), *Handbook of family therapy training and supervision* (pp. 237–251). New York: Guilford Press.

Frame, M. W. (2000). Constructing religious/spiritual genograms. In R. E. Watts (Ed.), *Techniques in marriage and family counseling* (pp. 69–74). Alexandria, VA: American Counseling Association.

Freedman, J., & Combs, G. (1996). *Narrative therapy*. New York: W. W. Norton.

Gergen, K. J. (1999). *An invitation to social construction*. London: Sage.

Gladding, S. T. (2002). *Family therapy: History, theory, and practice* (3rd ed.). Upper Saddle River, NJ: Merrill.

Goldner, V. (1993). Power and hierarchy: Let's talk about it! *Family Process, 32,* 157–162.

Gonçalves, O. (1995). Hermeneutics, constructivism and cognitive-behavioral therapies: From the object to the project. In R. A. Neimeyer & M. J. Mahoney (Eds.), *Constructivism in psychotherapy* (pp. 195–230). Washington, DC: American Psychological Association.

Goodman, G. Jr. (1972, March 24). Maya Angelou's lonely black outlook. *The New York Times*, p. 28.

Goolishian, H., & Anderson, A. (1987). Language systems and therapy: An evolving idea. *Psychotherapy, 24,* 529–545.

Grant, C. A., & Sleeter, C. E. (2002). *Turning on learning: Five approaches for multicultural teaching plans for race, class, gender, and disability*. New York: Wiley.

Green, J. B. (2003). *Introduction to family theory and therapy: Exploring an evolving field*. Pacific Grove, CA: Brooks/Cole.

Green, J. W. (1999). *Cultural awareness in the human services* (3rd ed.). Boston, MA: Allyn and Bacon.

Guerin, P. J., & Pendagast, E. G. (1976). Evaluations of family system and genogram. In P. J. Guerin (Ed.), *Family therapy: Theory and practice* (pp. 450–464). New York: Gardner Press.

Guidano, V. F. (1995). Self-observation in constructivist psychotherapy. In R. A. Neimeyer & M. J. Mahoney (Eds.), *Constructivism in psychotherapy* (pp. 61–84). Washington, DC: American Psychological Association.

Guterman, J. T. (1994). A social constructionist position for mental health counseling. *Journal of Mental Health Counseling, 16,* 226–244.

Hanson, S. M., & Boyd, S. (1996). *Family health care nursing*. Philadelphia: F. A. Davis.

Hardy, K. (1990). The theoretical myth of sameness: A critical issue in family therapy training and treatment. In G. Saba, B. Karrer, & K. Hardy (Eds.), *Minorities and family therapy* (pp. 17–33). New York: Haworth Press.

Hardy, K., & Laszloffy, T. (1995). The cultural genogram: Key to training culturally competent family therapists. *Journal of Marital and Family Therapy, 21,* 227–237.

Hare-Mustin, R. T. (1978). Discourses in the mirrored room: A postmodern analysis of therapy. *Family Process, 33,* 19–35.

Harland, R. (1987). *Superstructuralism*. London: Methuen.

Hartman, A. (1978). Diagrammatic assessment of family relationships. *Social Casework, 59,* 465–476.

Hayes, R. L. (1994). Counseling in the postmodern world: Origins and implications of a constructivist developmental approach. *Counseling and Human Development, 26*(6), 1–12.

Helms, J. (1990). *Black and White racial identity*. Westport, CT: Greenwood.

Hoffman, L. (1990). Constructing realities: An art of lenses. *Family Process, 29*, 1–12.

Howard, G. S. (1991). Cultural tales: A narrative approach to thinking, cross-cultural psychology and psychotherapy. *American Psychologist, 46*, 187–197.

Ibrahim, F. A. (1985). Effective cross-cultural counseling and psychotherapy: A framework. *Counseling Psychologist, 12*, 625–638.

Ivey, A. E. (1991). *Developmental strategies for helpers: Individual, family, and network interventions*. Pacific Grove, CA: Brooks/Cole.

Ivey, A. E. (1995). Psychotherapy as liberation. In J. Ponterotto, J. Casas, L. Suzuki, & C. Alexander (Eds.), *Handbook of multicultural counseling* (pp. 131–145). Beverly Hills, CA: Sage.

Ivey, A. E. (2000). *Developmental therapy: Theory into practice*. North Amherst, MA: Microtraining Associates.

Ivey, A. E., D'Andrea, M., Ivey, M. B., & Simek-Morgan, L. (2002). *Theories of counseling and psychotherapy: A multicultural perspective* (5th ed.). Boston: Allyn and Bacon.

Ivey, A. E., Gluckstern, N., & Ivey, M. (1992). *Basic attending skills* (3rd ed.). North Amherst, MA: Microtraining Associates.

Ivey, A. E., Gonçalves, O., & Ivey, M. (1989). Developmental therapy: Theory and practice. In O. Gonçalves (Ed.), *Advances in the cognitive therapies: The constructive-developmental approach* (pp. 91–110). Porto, Portugal: APPORT.

Ivey, A. E., Pedersen, P. B., & Ivey, M. B. (2001). *Intentional group counseling: A microskills approach*. Belmont, CA: Brooks/Cole.

Jackson, B. (1975). Black identity development. *Journal of Educational Diversity, 2*, 19–25.

Jackson, B. (1990). *Building a multicultural school*. Paper presented to the Amherst Regional School System, Amherst, MA.

Julianelli, J. (1972, November). Maya Angelou. *Harper's Bazaar*, p. 124.

Jung, C. (1935). The personal and collective unconscious. In C. Jung, *Collected works* (Vol. 7, pp. 87–110). New York: Pantheon.

Keeney, B. P. (1983). *Aesthetics of change*. New York: Guilford Press.

Kelly, G. A. (1955). *The psychology of personal constructs*. New York: Norton.

Kittredge, W. (1999). *Taking care: Thoughts on story-telling and belief*. Minneapolis, MN: Milkweed Editions.

L'Abate, L., & Bagarozzi, D. A. (1993). *Sourcebook of marriage and family evaluation*. New York: Bruner/Mazel.

Lambert, M., & Bergin, A. (1994). The effectiveness of psychotherapy. In A. Bergin & S. Garfield (Eds.), *Handbook of psychotherapy and behavior change* (pp. 184–197). New York: Wiley.

Locke, D. (1992). *Increasing multicultural understanding*. Beverly Hills, CA: Sage.

Luepnitz, D. (1988). *The family interpreted: Feminist theory in clinical practice*. New York: Basic Books.

Lyddon, W. J. (1995). Cognitive therapy and theories of knowing: A social constructionist view. *Journal of Counseling and Development, 73*, 579–585.

Mahoney, M. (2003). *Constructive psychotherapy: A practical guide*. New York: Guilford Press.

Martin, J. (1988). A proposal for researching possible relationships between scientific theories and the personal theories of counselors and clients. *Journal of Counseling and Development, 66,* 261–265.

Maturana, H., & Varela, F. (1987). *The tree of knowledge.* Boston: New Science Library.

McGoldrick, M., Gerson, R., & Shellenberger, S. (1999). *Genograms: Assessment and intervention* (2nd ed.). New York: W. W. Norton.

McLeod, J. (1997). *Narrative and psychotherapy.* London: Sage.

Meichenbaum, D. (1994). *A clinical handbook/practical therapist manual for assessing and treating adults with post-traumatic stress disorder (PTSD).* Waterloo, Ontario: Institute Press.

Meyerstein, I. (1979). The family behavioral snapshot: A tool for teaching family assessment. *American Journal of Family Therapy, 7,* 48–56.

Minuchin, S. (1974). *Families and family therapy.* Cambridge, MA: Harvard University Press.

Monk, G. (1997). How narrative therapy works. In G. Monk, J. Winslade, K. Crocket, & D. Epston (Eds.), *Narrative therapy in practice* (pp. 94–103). San Francisco: Jossey-Bass.

Montalvo, B. (1987). Family strengths: Obstacles and facilitators. In M. Karpel (Ed.), *Family resources: The hidden partner in family therapy* (pp. 93–115). New York: Guilford Press.

Morgan, A. (2000). *What is narrative therapy? An easy-to-read introduction.* Adelaide, South Australia: Dulwich Centre.

Mumford, D. J., & Weeks, G. (2003). The money genogram. *Journal of Family Psychotherapy, 14*(3), 33–44.

Neimeyer, G., & Neimeyer, R. A. (1994). Constructivist methods of marital and family therapy: A practical precis. *Journal of Mental Health Counseling, 116,* 85–104.

Neimeyer, R. A. (1998). Social constructionism in the counseling context. *Counseling Psychology Quarterly, 11,* 135–149.

Neimeyer, R., & Harter, S. (1988). Facilitating individual change in Personal Construct Therapy. In G. Dunnett (Ed.), *Working with people: Clinical use of Personal Construct Psychology* (pp. 83–97). London: Routledge.

Neimeyer, R. A., & Raskin, J. D. (Eds.). (2000). *Constructions of disorder: Meaning-making frameworks for psychotherapy.* Washington, DC: American Psychological Association.

Nieto, S. (2001). *Language, Culture and Teaching: Critical perspectives for a new century.* San Francisco: Lawrence Erlbaum.

Ogbonnaya, O. (1994). Person as community: An African understanding of the person as an intrapsychic community. *Journal of Black Psychology, 20,* 75–87.

O'Hanlon, W. H., & Weiner-Davis, M. (1989). *In search of solutions.* New York: W. W. Norton.

Paniagua, F. A. (2001). *Diagnosis in a multicultural context: A casebook for mental health professionals.* Thousand Oaks, CA: Sage.

Pedersen, P. (Ed.). (1991). Multiculturalism as a fourth force in counseling [Special issue]. *Journal of Counseling and Development, 70.*

Pedersen, P. (2000). *A handbook for developing multicultural awareness* (3rd ed.). Alexandria, VA: American Counseling Association.

Polkinghorne, D. E. (1994). Reaction to special section on qualitative research in counseling process and outcome. *Journal of Counseling Psychology, 41,* 510–512.

Ponterotto, J., Casas, J., Suzuki, L., & Alexander, C. (1995). *Handbook of multicultural counseling.* Beverly Hills, CA: Sage.

Prawat, R., & Floden, R. (1994). Philosophical perspectives on constructivist views of learning. *Educational Psychology, 29,* 37–48.

Rigazio-DiGilio, S. A. (1994). A co-constructive-developmental approach to ecosystemic treatment. *Journal of Mental Health Counseling, 16,* 43–74.

Rigazio-DiGilio, S. A. (1997). From microscopes to holographs: Client development within a constructivist paradigm. In T. Sexton & B. Griffin (Eds.), *Constructivist thinking in counseling practice, research, and training* (pp. 74–100). New York: Teachers College Press.

Rigazio-DiGilio, S. A. (2000). Reconstructing psychological distress and disorder from a relational perspective: A systemic coconstructive-developmental framework. In R. A. Neimeyer & J. D. Raskin (Eds.), *Constructions of disorder* (pp. 309–332). Washington, DC: American Psychological Association.

Rigazio-DiGilio, S. A., Gonçalves, O. F., & Ivey, A. E. (1996). From cultural to existential diversity: The impossibility of an integrative psychotherapy within a traditional framework. *Applied and Preventive Psychology: Current Scientific Perspectives, 5,* 235–248.

Rigazio-DiGilio, S. A., & Ivey, A. E. (1995). Individual and family issues in intercultural counselling and therapy: A culturally-centered perspective. *Canadian Journal of Counselling, 29,* 244–261.

Rigazio-DiGilio, S. A., Ivey, A. E., & Locke, D. (1997). Continuing the postmodern dialogue: Enhancing and contextualizing multiple voices. *Journal of Mental Health Counseling, 19,* 233–255.

Rogers, C. R. (1959). A theory and therapy, personality, and interpersonal relationships, as developed in the client-centered framework. In S. Koch (Ed.), *Psychology: A study of a science* (Vol. 3, pp. 97–109). New York: McGraw-Hill.

Rohner, R. (1986). *The warmth dimension: Foundations of parental acceptance-rejection theory.* New Perspectives on Family. San Francisco: Sage.

Seligman, M. S. P. (1975). *Helplessness: On depression, development, and death.* San Francisco: W. H. Freeman.

Sexton, T. L., & Whiston, S. C. (1994). The status of the counseling relationship: An empirical review, theoretical implications, and research directions. *Counseling Psychologist, 22,* 6–78.

Sloane, R., & Staples, F. (1984). Psychotherapy versus behavior therapy: Implications for future psychotherapy research. In J. Williams & R. Spitzer (Eds.), *Psychotherapy research: Where are we and where should we go?* (pp. 203–215). New York: Guilford Press.

Smith, G. P. (1998). *Common sense about uncommon knowledge: The knowledge bases for diversity*. Washington, DC: American Association of Colleges for Teacher Education (AACTE).

Sue, D. W., Ivey, A. E., & Pedersen, P. B. (1996). *A theory of multicultural counseling and therapy*. Pacific Grove, CA: Brooks/Cole.

Sue, D. W., & Sue, D. (1999). *Counseling the culturally different: Theory and practice* (3rd ed.). New York: Wiley.

Thomlison, B. (2002). *Family assessment handbook*. Pacific Grove, CA: Brooks/Cole.

Tomm, K. (1988). Interventive interviewing: III. Intending to ask lineal, circular, strategic, or reflective questions? *Family Process, 27,* 1–5.

Toppman, L. (1983, December 11). Maya Angelou: The serene spirit of a survivor. *Charlotte Observer,* pp. F1–2.

Von Foerster, H. (1984). On constructing a reality. In P. Watzlawick (Ed.), *The invented reality* (pp. 40–71). New York: W. W. Norton.

Von Glaserfeld, E. (1991). Knowing without metaphysics: Aspects of the radical constructivist position. In F. Steier (Ed.), *Research and reflexivity* (pp. 12–29). Knobbier Park, CA: Sage.

Vygotsky, L. (1986). *Thought and language*. Cambridge, MA: MIT Press. (Original work published 1934)

Watzlawick, P. (Ed.). (1984). *The invented reality*. New York: W. W. Norton.

Wentworth, W. M., & Wentworth, C. M. (1997). The social construction of culture and its implications for the therapeutic mind-self. In T. Sexton & B. Griffin (Eds.), *Constructivist thinking in counseling practice, research, and training* (pp. 41–57). New York: Teachers College Press.

Whipple, V. (1999). Feminist and family therapies: Continuing the dialogue. *ICA Quarterly, 147,* 2–13.

White, M. (1989). The externalizing of the problem. *Dulwich Centre Newsletter, 3*(20), 12, 15–16.

White, M. (1995). *Re-authorizing lives*. Adelaide, South Australia: Dulwich Centre.

White, M., & Epston, D. (1990). *Narrative means to therapeutic ends*. New York: Norton.

White, J., & Parham, T. (1991). *The psychology of Blacks: An African-American perspective*. Englewood Cliffs, NJ: Prentice-Hall.

Williams, R., & Wittig, M. A. (1997). "I'm not a feminist but . . .": Factors contributing to the discrepancy between pro-feminist orientation and feminist social identity. *Sex Roles, 37,* 885–904.

Wohl, J. (2000). Psychotherapy and cultural diversity. In J. Aponte & J. Wohl (Eds.), *Psychological intervention and cultural diversity* (2nd ed., pp. 75–90). Boston, MA: Allyn and Bacon.

Worden, M. (2003). *Family therapy basics* (3rd ed.). Pacific Grove, CA: Brooks/Cole.

Index

About the Authors and Contributor

AUTHORS

Sandra A. Rigazio-DiGilio, Ph.D., is a professor in the School of Family Studies / Marriage and Family Therapy Program, University of Connecticut, Storrs. She also is a licensed marriage and family therapist and psychologist. She has widely presented and published on an integrative, culturally and contextually based model of therapy, *Systemic Cognitive Developmental Therapy*, and its accompanying supervisory model, *Systemic Cognitive-Developmental Supervision*.

Allen E. Ivey, Ed.D., is a Distinguished University Professor (Emeritus) at the University of Massachusetts, Amherst. The author or coauthor of more than 35 books and 200 articles and chapters translated into at least 16 languages, he is the developer of microcounseling, the foundational skills training program, and developmental counseling and therapy (DCT).

Kara P. Kunkler-Peck, Ph.D., is a family therapist and special needs educator. She evaluates children at risk and implements educational programs for children with special needs while working closely with their families. She is actively involved with implementing antiracist curriculum and teaching strategies in the elementary school setting.

Lois T. Grady, Ph.D., received her undergraduate degree from Stanford University in economics in 1944 and completed graduate work in sociology at the University of Chicago while working for Educational Testing Service. She earned a master of fine arts in ceramics in 1971 and a doctorate in creative studies with a concentration in counseling psychology in 1989 at the University of Massachusetts. Her nature photographs, graphic work, and writing have appeared in numerous publications. She lives in Amherst, Massachusetts, with her husband of 58 years and their extended family, and is happily pursuing the study of geology and landscape.

CONTRIBUTOR

Anthony J. Rigazio-DiGilio, Ed.D., is professor and chair of the Department of Educational Leadership at Central Connecticut State University in New Britain, CT. He serves as a consultant to local, regional, national, and international groups interested in improving the organizational conditions that promote positive human interaction, teaching, leading, and learning.